TEACHER COMPETENCY TESTS

Elna M. Dimock

ARCO PUBLISHING, INC.
NEW YORK

First Edition, Second Printing, 1986

Published by Arco Publishing, Inc.
215 Park Avenue South, New York, NY 10003

Library of Congress Cataloging in Publication Data

Dimock, Elna M.
  Teacher competency tests.

  1. Examinations—Study guides.   2. Examinations—
Questions.   I. Title.
LB1762.D55   1985   370′.7′76   84-28346
ISBN 0-668-06231-2 (Paper Edition)

Printed in the United States of America

CONTENTS

GETTING THE MOST OUT OF THIS BOOK

Teaching is considered a portable skill, which is very convenient in our increasingly mobile society. And it used to be relatively easy to get a teaching position when moving from one state to another. But now, with the testing requirement for a teaching credential, all is confusion. More and more states require candidates for a credential to pass the state-designated test. The problem is that nearly all the tests are different. The plethora of tests makes it more difficult for a teacher in one state to get a credential to teach in another state.

Here is help! This book gives you information about each state: its testing requirements and the address and phone number of its credential or certification office. Directions are given about which parts of the review section you will need to study for each state and about which parts of the tests to practice. Finally, there are three sample tests, each of a different type.

HOW TO PROCEED

If you want a credential in a specific state

- Look the state up on page 5.
- Find the test requirements for that state.
- Call or write the state in order to

  double-check the requirements
  find out when the tests are given
  learn when you must sign up for the test and
    how long it takes to get the results
  ask for the forms and requirements to be sent.

- Sign up for the tests you need.

In this book, study test-taking techniques and the appropriate review sections. Take the practice tests, remembering to practice the test-taking techniques. Do your thinking with your pencil on the practice tests, just as you will on the test itself. Some tests do not allow scratch paper, so practicing in this book will pay big dividends. After you have corrected each test, study the explanations, turning to the review sections as necessary.

To see whether a state uses the National Teacher Examinations (NTE),* a state-developed or state-adopted basic skills test, a professional-knowledge test or none at all, turn to page 5.

*For a guide to these exams, see the 1984 edition of *NTE, National Teacher Examinations* by David J. Fox, Ph.D., from Arco Publishing of New York City.

1

STATE TEST REQUIREMENTS

The information in this book is as up-to-date as publishing deadlines allow. Do call the credential department of the state in which you wish to teach to make sure that requirements have not changed. The testing requirement has not passed in several states in which it was considered, but it may be brought up in the next session of the legislature. In several states in which it passed, the date for implementation was less than six months away.

This book deals only with testing requirements. In addition to degrees, some states require taking a class or passing a test in state school law, history or constitution.

State Departments of Education

ALABAMA	501 Dexter Avenue, Montgomery 36130 (205) 261-5060
ALASKA	Pouch F, Alaska Office Building, Juneau 99811 (907) 465-2810
ARIZONA	1535 West Jefferson Street, Phoenix 85007 (602) 255-4361
ARKANSAS	Education Building, Little Rock 72201 (501) 371-1474
CALIFORNIA	721 Capitol Mall, Sacramento 95814 (916) 445-4338
COLORADO	201 East Colfax Avenue, #523, Denver 80203 (303) 534-8871
CONNECTICUT	165 Capitol Avenue, P.O. Box 2219, Hartford 06115 (203) 566-4561
DELAWARE	State Department of Public Instruction, P.O. Box 1402, Dover 19901 (302) 736-4686
DISTRICT OF COLUMBIA	Public Schools of the District of Columbia, 415 12th Street North West, Washington 20004 (202) 724-4230
FLORIDA	PL08, Capitol Building, Tallahassee 32301 (904) 487-1785
GEORGIA	Twin Towers East, Suite 2066, 205 Butler Street Southeast, Atlanta 30334 (404) 656-2604
HAWAII	P.O. Box 2360, Honolulu 96804 (808) 548-5804
IDAHO	Len B. Jordan Building, Boise 83720 (208) 334-3475
ILLINOIS	100 North First Street, Springfield 62777 (217) 782-4321
INDIANA	State Department of Public Instruction, State House, Room 229, Indianapolis 46204 (317) 232-6636

IOWA	State Department of Public Instruction, Grimes State Office Building, Des Moines 50319 (515) 281-3245
KANSAS	120 East Tenth Street, Topeka 66612 (913) 296-2288
KENTUCKY	Capitol Plaza Tower, Frankfort 40601 (502) 564-4606
LOUISIANA	626 North Fourth Street, P.O. Box 44064, Baton Rouge 70804 (504) 342-3490
MAINE	State Department of Education and Cultural Services, State House Station No. 23, Augusta 04333 (207) 289-2441
MARYLAND	200 West Baltimore Street, Baltimore 21201 (301) 659-2134
MASSACHUSETTS	Quincy Center Plaza, 1385 Hancock Street, Quincy 02169 (617) 770-7517
MICHIGAN	P.O. Box 30008, Lansing 48909 (517) 373-3324
MINNESOTA	712 Capitol Square Building, 550 Cedar Street, St. Paul 55101 (612) 296-2046
MISSISSIPPI	P.O. Box 771, Jackson 39205 (601) 359-3483
MISSOURI	State Department of Elementary and Secondary Education, P.O. Box 480, Jefferson State Office Building, Jefferson City 65102 (314) 751-4212
MONTANA	Office of Public Instruction, State Capitol, Room 106, Helena 59620 (406) 444-2511
NEBRASKA	P.O. Box 94987, 301 Centennial Mall South, Lincoln 68509 (402) 471-2295
NEVADA	400 West King Street, Carson City 89710 (702) 885-3115
NEW HAMPSHIRE	410 State House Annex, Concord 03301 (603) 271-1110
NEW JERSEY	C.N. 500, 225 West State Street, Trenton 08625 (609) 292-4477
NEW MEXICO	State Capitol, Santa Fe 87501 (505) 827-6587
NEW YORK	Education Building, Albany 12234 (518) 474-3901
NORTH CAROLINA	State Department of Public Instruction, Education Building, Raleigh 27611 (919) 733-4125
NORTH DAKOTA	State Department of Public Instruction, State Capitol Building, 600 Boulevard Avenue East, Bismarck 58505 (701) 224-2264
OHIO	65 South Front Street, Columbus 43215 (614) 466-3593
OKLAHOMA	Oliver Hodge Memorial Education Building, 2500 North Lincoln Boulevard, Oklahoma City 73105 (405) 521-3337
OREGON	700 Pringle Parkway Southeast, Salem 97310 (503) 378-3569
PENNSYLVANIA	333 Market Street, Box 911, Harrisburg 17108 (717) 787-2967
RHODE ISLAND	22 Hayes Street, Providence 02908 (401) 277-2675
SOUTH CAROLINA	1006 Rutledge Building, 1429 Senate Street, Columbia 29201 (803) 758-5081
SOUTH DAKOTA	Kneip Building, Pierre 57501 (605) 773-3553
TENNESSEE	100 Cordell Hull Building, Nashville 37219 (615) 741-1644

TEXAS	Texas Education Agency, 201 East 11th Street, Austin 78701 (512) 834-4122
UTAH	State Office of Education, 250 East Fifth, South, Salt Lake City 84111 (801) 533-5965
VERMONT	120 State Street, Montpelier 05602 (802) 828-2445
VIRGINIA	P.O. Box 6–Q, Richmond 23216 (804) 225-2097
WASHINGTON	State Department of Public Instruction, 7510 Armstrong Street Southwest, Tumwater 98504 (206) 753-6717
WEST VIRGINIA	1900 Washington Street, Charleston 25305 (304) 348-2681
WISCONSIN	State Department of Public Instruction, 125 South Webster Street, Box 7841, Madison 53707 (608) 266-1027
WYOMING	Hathaway Building, Cheyenne 82002 (307) 777-6261

SUMMARY OF TEST REQUIREMENTS

KEY TO CHART

1 = no test
2 = test required
3 = test requirement under consideration
4 = NTE (National Teacher Examinations) core battery required
5 = NTE specialty examinations required
6 = state-developed or state-adopted basic-skills test required
7 = state-developed or state-adopted professional-knowledge test required
8 = state teaching specialty test required
9 = test required for entrance to education programs at state colleges and universities
10 = special requirements, see state section that follows

State	1	2	3	4	5	6	7	8	9	10
AL		✔				✔	✔	✔		
AK	✔									
AZ		✔				✔	✔			
AR		✔		✔	✔					✔
CA		✔		✔	✔	✔				
CO		✔								✔
CT		✔					✔	✔	✔	
DC	✔									
DE		✔				✔				
FL		✔				✔	✔			
GA		✔				✔	✔			
HI			✔							
ID	✔									
IL	✔									
IN		✔				✔	✔	✔		
IA	✔									
KS			✔							
KY		✔		✔						✔
LA		✔		✔	✔					
ME	✔									
MD		✔		✔	✔				✔	

State	1	2	3	4	5	6	7	8	9	10
MA	✔									
MI	✔									
MN	✔									
MS		✔		✔	✔					
MO	✔								✔	
MT			✔							
NE		✔				✔		✔	✔	
NV	✔									
NH	✔									
NJ			✔							
NM		✔		✔	✔					
NY		✔			✔					
NC		✔		✔	✔					
ND	✔									
OH			✔							
OK		✔						✔		
OR		✔				✔				
PA			✔							
RI	✔									
SC		✔			✔					
SD	✔									
TN		✔		✔						
TX		✔							✔	✔
UT			✔							
VT	✔									
VA		✔		✔	✔					
WA			✔							
WV		✔								✔
WI	✔									
WY		✔								✔

ABOUT STATES THAT REQUIRE TESTS

ALABAMA You must pass an English proficiency test (essay, listening, reading, composition, grammar) to enter an education program in state colleges. The certification test has two parts: a basic professional-study test of 120 multiple-choice questions, which takes three hours in the morning, and an equally long test in the afternoon on your teaching field (elementary, English, physics, etc.). The test is given three times a year, in September, December and March. Register a minimum of five weeks before the test. The cost for one part is $35, $58 for both parts.

ARIZONA The Arizona Teacher Proficiency Exam is given weekly in Phoenix, monthly in Tucson and Flagstaff. The sign-up deadline is two weeks before the examination, but register early to get your first choice of date and place. The cost is $10. The basic skills test (reading, mathematics and grammar) takes 130 minutes and has 150 questions. The professional-knowledge test of 73 questions takes 90 minutes. You will get your scores in about two weeks.

ARKANSAS A commission appointed by the governor is studying testing requirements for teachers now employed and credentialed. Will they have to pass a test of functional academic skills or the NTE, take six semester units in their subject area or take a subject-area test?

CALIFORNIA The California Basic Educational Skills Test (CBEST) is required for earning an initial credential, for renewing a provisional credential and for getting a different credential. It is given five times a year, in February, April, July, September and December. Sign up at least five weeks before the test. The cost is $32. The reading, mathematics and writing portions of the test each take about one hour. The required total score is 123, with no score lower than 37. It will be about five weeks before you receive your scores.

COLORADO The California Achievement Test (level 19, form C or D) is used for initial certification. It tests reading, mathematics, spelling and grammar. You must either demonstrate your ability to express yourself in oral English before a panel of judges or document that you have passed a college course in public speaking with a grade of B or higher. The test is administered at colleges in Colorado. Contact the college where you will be taking the test for more information.

CONNECTICUT A state test is to be developed. Beginning May, 1985, there will be an entry test to teacher-preparation programs. It will cover the basic skills in mathematics, reading and writing. In May, 1987, there will be a teacher-program exit test on professional knowledge and a certification examination in the candidate's subject area.

DELAWARE The following scores on the Pre-Professional Skills Test are required for initial certification: reading 175, writing 175, mathematics 172. The test takes three hours and costs $25. It is given at three colleges in October, March and June. Register at least three weeks before the examination date at the college most convenient for you.

FLORIDA The Florida Teacher Certification Examination is required for a credential. The test is given three times a year in October, February and June at several locations. The registration deadline is eleven weeks before the test. The test takes all day; writing, reading and mathematics are tested in the morning and professional knowledge in the afternoon. The cost is $12. You will receive your scores in about two months.

GEORGIA The Georgia Teacher Certification Program is required of almost all candidates for initial certification. If you want an evaluation of your status, send all your information to the Department of Education and allow at least a month for the evaluation. Professional-knowledge tests are given in each of twenty-eight areas and include writing, math and reading. You may take tests in two areas in a single day, but you must send in separate registrations ($35 each). The tests are given at almost all Georgia colleges in February, May and November. Sign up at least five weeks ahead of the test date. Registration information is available from the Department of Education. Testing is being considered for current teachers.

HAWAII A testing requirement is being considered by the state's Teacher Education Coordinating Committee.

INDIANA A test of your general-education, professional-education, communication-skills and subject-area knowledge is required for initial certification.

KANSAS The core battery of the National Teacher Examinations is under consideration for initial certification.

KENTUCKY The California Test of Basic Skills (CTBS) is required for entry to educational programs. Teachers obtaining an initial credential or teachers from out of state with less than five years of experience must take the NTE and will intern for a year. During that year they will be assisted and evaluated by a three-member team. Upon successful completion of the year they will receive a regular credential.

LOUISIANA The NTE core-battery test is required with the following scores: communication 645, general knowledge 644, professional knowledge 645. The scores needed for the specialty areas vary.

MARYLAND The Pre-Professional Skills Test is required for entrance to education programs. The NTE core-battery test and the area-specialty test are required as exit tests, which are equivalent to initial-certification tests.

MISSISSIPPI The NTE core battery test is required with the following scores: communication 641, general knowledge 636, professional knowledge 639. The passing score on the area-specialty tests varies.

MISSOURI There is no certification test now. Each college has its own entrance test to the education program.

MONTANA A testing requirement is under consideration.

NEBRASKA The entry test to the education program covers basic skills (usually reading, mathematics, writing or grammar). There is a subject-area exit test.

NEW JERSEY A test, to be developed, is proposed for the fall of 1985.

NEW MEXICO The core-battery test of the NTE is required for certification. Passing scores are: communication 644, general knowledge 645, professional knowledge 630. Specialty-area tests are required beginning fall, 1985.

NEW YORK The core-battery test of the NTE is required for certification. Required scores are: communication 650, general knowledge 649, professional knowledge 646.

NORTH CAROLINA The professional-knowledge part of the NTE is required. If it is available, the area-specialty exam is also required.

OKLAHOMA The Oklahoma Teacher Competency Proficiency Test, a state-developed test, is required for a teaching credential. It tests specialty areas and is administered four times a year at various locations in the state. Sign up a month before the test date. The cost of the tests varies, and the exam takes two days, a Saturday and Sunday. It may be retaken.

OREGON The state has adopted the California Basic Educational Skills Test (CBEST). The test is given five times a year, in February, April, July, September and December. Sign up at least five weeks before the test date. The cost is $32. The reading, mathematics and writing portions of the test each take about an hour. The required total score is 123, with no single score being lower than 37. You will receive your score in about five weeks.

PENNSYLVANIA A task force is working on developing a test.

SOUTH CAROLINA The Educational Entrance Examination (EEE), a basic skills test, is required for entrance to the teacher-education program. It is administered by the individual colleges. The NTE specialty-area exam is used as an exit test. Required scores vary.

TENNESSEE The NTE is used.

TEXAS The Pre-Professional Skills Test (PPST) is used on sixty-two college campuses as the entrance test to teacher programs. It can be taken three times a year, in the fall, spring and summer. Sign up at the college most convenient for you. To obtain a credential you must pass a test in Texas government, history and constitution. This requirement applies to teachers with out-of-state credentials, too. As of fall, 1986, there will be an exit test.

UTAH A testing requirement is under consideration.

VIRGINIA The NTE core-battery and area-specialty exams are now required, but there are no scores specified for certification. However, beginning in July of 1986, a candidate wishing an initial certification must achieve scores on the three core-battery tests as follows: communication 649, professional knowledge 639, general knowledge 639. Passing scores for the area-specialty exams vary from one examination to another.

WASHINGTON A bill requiring testing for a teaching credential was considered by the state legislature in the spring of 1984. It did not pass but may come up again.

WEST VIRGINIA The NTE or the Graduate Record Examination is required of graduates of West Virginia institutions. Score-level requirements vary with each institution. Teachers with out-of-state credentials do not need to meet this requirement.

WYOMING You must pass a test on the Wyoming constitution to obtain a teaching credential.

WHICH SECTIONS OF THIS BOOK
TO STUDY FOR YOUR TEST

ALABAMA
: Test-Taking Techniques
Review: Professional Knowledge
Sample Test 2: Professional Knowledge
Sample Test 3: Professional Knowledge

ARIZONA
: Test-Taking Techniques
Review: Reading, Mathematics, Grammar, Professional Knowledge
Sample Test 2: Reading, Mathematics, Grammar, Professional Knowledge
Sample Test 3: Professional Knowledge

CALIFORNIA
: Test-Taking Techniques
Review: Reading, Mathematics, Writing
Sample Test 1: Reading, Mathematics, Writing

COLORADO
: Test-Taking Techniques
Review: Mathematics, Grammar
Sample Test 1: Mathematics
Sample Test 2: Mathematics, Grammar
Sample Test 3: Mathematics

CONNECTICUT
(entry test)
: Test-Taking Techniques
Review: Reading, Mathematics, Writing
Sample Test 1: Reading, Mathematics, Writing

DELAWARE
: Test-Taking Techniques
Review: Reading, Mathematics, Writing
Sample Test 1: Reading, Mathematics, Writing

FLORIDA
: Test-Taking Techniques
Review: Reading, Mathematics, Writing, Professional Knowledge
Sample Test 2: Professional Knowledge
Sample Test 3: Writing, Reading, Mathematics, Professional Knowledge

GEORGIA
: Test-Taking Techniques
Review: Reading, Mathematics, Writing, Professional Knowledge
Sample Test 1: Reading, Mathematics, Writing
Sample Test 2: Reading, Mathematics, Professional Knowledge
Sample Test 3: Writing, Reading, Mathematics, Professional Knowledge

INDIANA
: Test-Taking Techniques
Review: Reading, Mathematics, Grammar, Writing, Professional Knowledge

Sample Test 2: Reading, Mathematics, Grammar, Professional
    Knowledge
Sample Test 3: Professional Knowledge

KENTUCKY	Test-Taking Techniques Review: Reading, Mathematics, Grammar Sample Test 2: Reading, Mathematics, Grammar
MARYLAND	Test-Taking Techniques Review: Reading, Mathematics, Writing Sample Test 1: Reading, Mathematics, Writing
MISSOURI (*entry test*)	Test-Taking Techniques Review: Reading, Mathematics, Writing Sample Test 1: Reading, Mathematics, Writing
NEBRASKA	Test-Taking Techniques Review: Reading, Mathematics, Grammar Sample Test 1: Reading, Mathematics Sample Test 2: Reading, Mathematics, Grammar Sample Test 3: Reading, Mathematics
OREGON	Test-Taking Techniques Review: Reading, Mathematics, Writing Sample Test 1: Reading, Mathematics, Writing
PENNSYLVANIA	Test-Taking Techniques Review: Reading, Mathematics, Writing Sample Test 1: Reading, Mathematics, Writing
SOUTH CAROLINA (*entry test*)	Test-Taking Techniques Review: Reading, Mathematics, Writing, Grammar Sample Test 1: Reading, Mathematics, Writing Sample Test 2: Reading, Mathematics, Grammar Sample Test 3: Writing, Reading, Mathematics
TEXAS	Test-Taking Techniques Review: Reading, Mathematics, Writing Sample Test 1: Reading, Mathematics, Writing

TEST-TAKING TECHNIQUES

GENERAL

Your score on a test depends on how much you know, your level of test anxiety and your test-taking skills. This section will help you master your anxiety and improve your skills. The knowledge requirement is handled in the review chapter.

TEST ANXIETY

There are a few people who don't experience test anxiety. Lucky for them! For the rest of us, test anxiety manifests itself in many forms—from sweaty palms, inability to eat, digestion problems and lumps in the throat to memory loss and paralysis. It is no laughing matter. You may not be able to get rid of test anxiety entirely, but it can be tamed. A bit of it can keep you alert. Here is what you can do.

Prepare for the test psychologically. Imagine the scene: You arrive at the test site. You're in plenty of time. You have all your supplies with you. You meet people who are there to take the test, too. What will they say? "I'm so nervous. Aren't you?" "I heard this was the worst test. No one passes." You cannot control others completely, but you can control your reactions and responses. Sometimes people who are negative are trying to make you as nervous as they are. You don't need to play their ain't-it-awful game. You can say, "No, I'm not nervous." You can ignore them or walk away or say, "I'd rather not talk right now. I'll talk to you later." Your job now is to protect yourself and keep positive images. What they do is unimportant. How you react inwardly is all-important.

Now you walk into the room, get checked off the master list, go to your assigned place and sit down. There is no rush, because you have plenty of time.

Be an island of calm. Don't let the nervous atmosphere penetrate your invisible shield. You're here to do your very best. This test can get you a credential that will be professionally and financially rewarding. Relax; look around you. You have energy and confidence. Other peoples' problems are not yours right now. Disturbances are all outside your shield and don't enter your calm world.

TEST-TAKING SKILLS

RELAXATION TECHNIQUES

Practice the following techniques to avoid tension and gain serenity. It's important to practice these before the test so that you will use them automatically during the test.

Escape. Close your eyes and take a mini-vacation. Picture the calmest environment possible—the beach, the mountains, a garden. Picture yourself there. Enjoy the tranquillity. After fifteen to thirty seconds you will open your eyes, feeling relaxed and refreshed.

Breathe slowly, breathing out all tension.

Unkink your muscles. Stretch your legs and relax. Rotate your ankles. Stretch your arms forward and relax them. Clench your fists and relax them. Rotate your shoulders to release the tension in the muscles between your shoulder blades. Close your eyes and roll your head on your neck, four times to the right and four times to the left. These techniques are useful any time, not just during the test.

BEFORE THE TEST

Several days before the test, check the test site out. How long does it take to get there? Where do you park? Where is the testing room? Where are the rest rooms?

Get happy. Avoid arguments and depressing situations if possible. Get rid of any anger you may have, or at least put it on the shelf for the time being. If you have a friend who always has problems and always "shares" them, stay away from that friend the week before the test. Worry only about what is real and what you can do something about. Anything else is unproductive. Anger and worry drain a great deal of energy. You need that energy for the test.

The night before the test, follow your regular routine. Don't do any special studying. Most of all, you need a clear head for thought and analysis. Have ready what you need for the test: #2 pencils, eraser, pen, admission ticket, identification, watch, perhaps a sweater. If the test is very long, take a snack or lunch.

The morning of the test, eat lightly or as usual. Don't take any artificial stimulants or relaxants.

Wear comfortable, layered clothing that can be put on or taken off as necessary for comfort. Do not dress sloppily or too casually or you won't do your best.

Arrive thirty minutes early to give yourself plenty of time to park, get to the room, and get checked in without rushing.

If you have a choice of seats, sit where you can concentrate—not by a door, aisle, pencil sharpener or distracting people. If you're left-handed, request a left-handed desk. You may not get it, but it doesn't hurt to ask.

DURING THE TEST

Be enthusiastic. This test is your means to the credential you want.

Use the relaxation techniques while the test administrator reads the directions. They are very helpful. Expect the preliminaries to take half an hour. During the test, breathe slowly. Relax and unkink your muscles every half hour, using the techniques you have practiced. Escape on your mini-vacation every hour or whenever you feel your eyes crossing or the words blurring.

Don't let others bother you. If someone near you sighs as though he's dying or another writes and erases furiously, just block them out. Don't let their problems become yours. Think only of doing your best. You know a lot more than you think you do. You know what to expect.

Keep on going; don't get bored. This is a game of sorts—a game you will win. It's worth the effort.

MECHANICS OF TEST-TAKING

Be sure your name and all supplementary information are correct. Even though you are familiar with the directions, read them carefully.

Mark machine-scored answer sheets carefully and completely. Outline $\bigcirc$, then fill in ◑ ● Erasures should be complete.

PACING YOURSELF

When the proctor says you may start, write the time on the answer sheet at question 1. Add half the time allotted for the section, or a little less, and write that time at the middle question. Write the ending time at the last question. When you get to the halfway point as you work on the test, you can check the time to see whether you are ahead of or behind schedule. This system allows some review time at the end. You will not need to look at your watch all the time, either. Erase the times on your answer sheet before you hand your test in.

INSURANCE

Before you start the test, mark the last ten answers in the section with the same letter (all Bs or Cs, for instance). Thus, if you haven't finished when the time is up, you have at least one chance in four or five of getting the last ten correct. If you don't mark them, you have no chance. As you work through the test and come to the last questions, you can readily change the answers. Remember, there is no penalty for guessing.

TACKLING A QUESTION

You have paid for the test. Unless you are given scratch paper, write, mark and solve problems on the test.

Read the questions carefully. Don't jump to conclusions. Does it say *must* or *may*, *and* or *or*, *always* or *sometimes*? Break complicated questions into parts. Check your answer against each part. Underline key words.

Example:

12. The fraction $^{12}/_{11}$ is between the numbers
     given in each of the following pairs except

Underline *between* and *except*.

You may sometimes find it useful to cross out the answers that you can easily see are unlikely or impossible.

Example:

5. $\sqrt{31}$ is between

    (A) 100 and 1,000
    (B) 3 and 4
    (C) 5 and 6
    (D) 15 and 16
    (E) 60 and 64

The square root of 31 must be less than 31. Eliminate A and E. Answer D is half of 31, which is unlikely.

If you cannot decide between two answers, choose one, circle it and put a mark by the number of the question.

−5. $\sqrt{31}$ is between

    (A) 100 and 1,000
    (B) 3 and 4
    (C) 5 and 6
    (D) 15 and 16
    (E) 60 and 64

Indicate your choice on the answer sheet, and put a mark by the number.

```
        A   B   C   D   E
   − 5  ○   ○   ●   ○   ○
```

Don't leave an answer unmarked. You will lose your place more easily if you do, as well as missing a chance to get the right answer.

A question must earn your time and attention. If you haven't decided on an answer after one minute, mark it as above and go on. If you have no idea what the answer is, choose B or C or D, but not the same letter as the answer just above or just below. Don't leave an answer blank. The mark by the number shows that you should go back to it after you have finished the section, if you have enough time. If the question is a super-puzzler, put two marks by it. There are only a few two-mark questions. As you review each questionable answer, look only at the choices not crossed out. Make your decision, and *erase* the mark by the number of the question on the answer sheet. Do the super-puzzlers (two marks) last. Since all the questions count equally, spend your time on those that are easiest for you. It's not a good idea to spend five minutes on a single question when in the same time you could be answering five questions.

When you guess, avoid such answers as "none of the above" and "it cannot be determined." They are usually put in when the test-maker cannot think of another choice. Of course, they must be correct once in a while, just to keep you guessing, but the averages are against it.

If you have a choice of combinations of numbered answers, and you're not sure of the answer, choose the one with the number that is used most often in the answers.

Example:

    (A) I
    (B) II
    (C) III
    (D) II and III
    (E) I and II

I is used two times. II is used three times. III appears twice. The best guess is B.

Work quickly, but not hastily. Mark your answers carefully. Go over the test after you have finished, making sure that all your answers are in the right spaces. Return to those questions you checked for further thought. Reread the directions, questions and answers. Check your calculations. Don't be afraid to change an answer. *Erase all extra marks on the answer sheet.* Check identical answers on successive questions carefully, especially if there are three or more in a row.

STRATEGIES FOR SPECIFIC QUESTIONS

READING

You will read a short passage, from one sentence to several paragraphs. There will be from one to five questions after each passage. First, quickly read the stems of the questions that pertain to the passage.

Example:

13. The most appropriate title is

> (A) Clarity
> (B) The Placement of Modifiers
> (C) The Purpose of Writing
> (D) The First Rule
> (E) Ideals

"The most appropriate title is" constitutes the stem of the question.

Decide whether the question involves interpretation or facts. Put I for interpretation or F for facts by the question.

Then read the passage carefully, keeping the questions in mind. Underline key words as you go, especially those that present facts. Answer as many of the questions as you can. Then reread the passage and answer the remaining questions. If absolutely necessary, read the paragraph a third time. Take your best shot at the remaining questions. Remember the marking technique.

Check the answer. Refer back to the sentence that supports the answer to be sure it is correct. Be certain the answer covers all parts of the question.

Don't add facts you happen to know. The questions test your ability to read and understand *only* a given passage. Forget your own conclusions.

Don't expect to find the answer to an inferential question stated word for word in a passage.

Don't pick a specific answer when a general one is asked for.

If you are still unsure about a question even after three readings of the passage, don't return to it unless you have extra time at the end. It takes too long to reread the passage.

SENTENCE COMPLETION

As you read the sentence, look for clues in its structure or rhythm that tell you what kinds of words will be best suited for filling in the blanks. Watch for key words in the sentence. Guess at the answer even before consulting the choices. One choice will likely match or approximate your guess.

Look for clue words that indicate the blanks have contrasting meanings. For example, *not . . . but, rather than* and *whereas*. Be alert to clues of similarity, such as *not only . . . but also* and *as well as*.

The part of the sentence without the blank will often define or suggest what the missing word should be. Start with that part of the sentence and work backward.

When there are two blanks and you don't find an answer choice that fits the first one, try to find choices that fit the second one. Then go back to the first blank.

MATHEMATICS

Read each question carefully, so that you solve for what is asked. Estimate the answer first, then work it out. Do all of your work on the test, unless scratch paper is provided. Cross out answers that are not possible. This narrows your choices and may leave you with only one answer.

Study graphs carefully. Are they to scale?

Round amounts off when you're asked for an approximate answer.

Draw a diagram or sketch and label it.

Check your calculations. Copy correctly. Make your work columns and figures neat to avoid errors. Work quickly, but don't get sloppy.

Watch for mixed units of measure in the questions and answers. Eliminate answers with wrong units and, when in doubt, those with the highest and lowest figures.

When a question asks you to find an exception, look for some element common to all the choices except one. The choice without that element is your answer.

You can try each answer out to see whether it works in the question. Usually there is a very simple or short-cut solution. Be alert for it.

Most of your mistakes will be due to carelessness in reading, not to your inability to do the math. Reread the question. Triple check the problem if there is time.

What to do if you don't have any idea what the answer is:

If all the answer choices form a series, such as 4, 6, 8, 10, 12, avoid the extremes: 4 and 12. If you are to find the largest number that will work, pick the largest or next-to-largest number. Remember, there is no penalty for guessing.

WRITING

The topics draw from your personal observations and experiences. The topics are analytical or expressive. They are usually changed each time the tests are given. Everyone taking the test on the same day ordinarily writes on the same topic(s).

Spend ten minutes on each topic, organizing your thoughts.

Do not stray from the topic title, or your essay will not count. If you don't like the topic and think you could write a better essay on another topic, resist the impulse.

Support your generalizations with specific examples. Be as specific and concrete as possible.

Write with care and precision. Scoring is based on organization, flow, cohesiveness, focus on the subject matter, level of vocabulary, strength of supporting arguments, mechanics and style.

One essay You will have forty-five minutes to write on one of two topics. Write on the topic with which you are most comfortable.

Two essays You will be asked to write about two topics in sixty minutes. Spend thirty minutes on each or twenty minutes on one and forty minutes on the other. Write on the topic that you feel most comfortable about first.

GRAMMAR

Generally, choose the answer that "sounds" best to you. Remember that the grammar being tested is written, not spoken usage; therefore, the language will be somewhat formal. Beware, however, of sentences that sound too formal.

PROFESSIONAL KNOWLEDGE

Some questions are factual, and you'll choose the answer you've learned or the one that seems most logical.

When questions deal with opinion, keep in mind current attitudes of educators and administrators. When in doubt, ask yourself: Which answer will benefit the child most? Which answer asks everyone's opinion? Which answer gets the most people involved?

REVIEW OF SKILLS
AND KNOWLEDGE

READING REVIEW

The questions in the reading section are designed to test your ability to interpret, analyze and evaluate a reading passage. You do not need to draw on outside knowledge. Work only with what is stated or implied in the passage.

Familiarize yourself with the main categories of reading questions:

> Interpreting a passage
> Drawing inferences
> Drawing conclusions
> Knowing the meanings of specific words
> Paraphrasing a portion of the text
> Determining what the next sentence might be
> Applying the information in the passage to another situation
> Determining the main idea
> Completing a sentence
> Analyzing a graph

The length of the passages varies from one sentence to several paragraphs. There are from one to five questions after each passage. If you are short of time toward the end of the test, it is better to read two short passages and answer one question about each than it is to tackle a long passage and not have time to answer any of the accompanying questions.

TYPES OF QUESTIONS

1. **Fill in a word (or words) to complete the sentence.**

Example:

38. Blue is a calming color. Men may fish, not so much for the _____ but for the _____ of the stream and sky.

    (A) sport . . . excitement
    (B) thrill . . . movement
    (C) fish . . . action
    (D) excitement . . . tumbling
    (E) catch . . . serenity

Strategy. Before looking at your answer choices:

Read the sentence through, filling in your own words. Choose simple words.

Then look at the answer choices and decide whether any of them are synonyms or fit with your words.

Try each set of words out in the sentence. Remember, the sentence must flow. If the sentence is written in an erudite style, the missing words will be complex. If the sentence is colloquial, the words will be simple.

If there is more than one word to be filled in, look at the first word of the choices and eliminate those that don't fit. In the above example, they all fit.

Go on to the second word. Which words don't fit? *Excitement, movement, action* and *tumbling* don't fit with *calming* in the sentence. We are now left with E. Note that this passage has a *not . . . but* construction.

Read the sentence again, incorporating the words from E to see whether it makes sense.

If at any point during this process you hit on the right answer, mark it and go on.

2. **Choose the most logical interpretation.** Notice the word *most*. There may be several interpretations that fit, but you need to find the most obvious one, or the one you think the testmakers had in mind. This is no time for innovative thinking.

Example:

7. The expressionist painters at the turn of the century tried to depict a state of mind rather than to make a realistic copy of some object.

    (A) Expressionist paintings resemble camera snapshots.
    (B) Most expressionist paintings are of people.
    (C) Expressionist paintings are all done in oils.
    (D) Expressionist paintings give the feeling rather than the appearance of things.
    (E) Expressionist paintings are all done in pastels.

Strategy. When you have read the sentence, underline the key points:

state of mind and *realistic copy*

You might even write *not* above *rather than*. The idea is "state of mind not copy." As you read each possible answer, draw a line through the ones that don't fit your conclusion. Then (A) is eliminated. Choices (B), (C) and (E) may be true, but no mention is made of these things in the passage. Choice (D) is best. *Feeling* takes the place of *state of mind* and *appearance* takes the place of *copy*.

3. **Determine the main idea.** This question can appear in several forms, such as: "Choose a title." "What is the central thought?" "What would a good topic sentence be?" "The author's purpose is . . . ." "The theme is . . . ." "This passage illustrates . . . ." The key to this type of question is that the answer you choose must be comprehensive. Choose the answer that is supported by the whole passage.

Example:

1   The physical language of time and space—movement, rhythm and
2   pacing—is a language that communicates a world of significance,
3   especially, perhaps, to preschool children, who are still more
4   fluent in body language than in verbal language. One way people
5   stand or move may mutely signal importance, intimacy, or consent:
6   another may indicate that the relationship is distant or that consent
7   is to be withheld or that the goings-on are unimportant,
8   peripheral to the main event. Children must learn the spatial
9   codes for their own and other cultures. Playacting—their own and
10   dramatizations they watch—is essential to this learning.

24. The information in the passage suggests
    that preschool teachers should be particu-
    larly aware of messages they communicate
    by their

    (A) tone of voice
    (B) movements and gestures
    (C) choice of words
    (D) choice of group discussion topics
    (E) scheduling of activities for the day

Throughout the passage nonverbal or body language is discussed. Choice E is completely out. Choices A, C and D are all verbal. Choice B, a synonym for body language, is correct.

Strategy

  Read the stem of the question.
  Read the passage through as fast as you can to get an over-all feel for it. What is
  your general impression?
  Read the answer choices. Eliminate any that don't fit.
  Read the passage again for refinement.
  Underline key points with your pencil or just note them with your eyes as you read
  the passage.
  Does one of the answers fit? Good. If not, eliminate answers that deal with only
  part of the passage.
  Does your final choice deal with the whole topic?

    4. Infer. Inferential questions ask you to deduce something from the passage.
       You must understand the passage clearly to make inferences. Read the
       passage at the top of this page and use it to answer the following question.

Example:

25. It can be inferred from the passage that
    which of the following is true of spatial
    codes?

    (A) They are less easily understood by pre-
        school children than by older children.
    (B) They are most effectively learned in
        the classroom.
    (C) They differ from culture to culture.

(D) They function in written as well as nonverbal communication.

(E) They are more frequently used to signal important rather than unimportant relationships.

Use elimination to find the answer.

(A) no—line 3
(B) no—lines 3 and 4
(C) maybe—lines 8 and 9
(D) no—lines 1, 2 and 4
(E) no—lines 5 through 7. They are used for both important and unimportant relationships.

The answer is C, since none of the other choices qualifies.

5. **Determine the meaning of words** as used in the text. Remember that you need to give the meaning as it is used in this particular passage. Even though you may know one meaning of a word, it may not be the one used in this passage.

Example:

9. The shell *evoked* sounds of the sea.

Evoked in this sentence means

(A) recreated
(B) made
(C) brought to mind
(D) muffled
(E) simulated

Strategy

Read the stem and underline *evoked*.
Read the passage and underline *evoked*. *Evoke* means "to bring forth from memory." Choice D doesn't fit at all. Choice C is closest.

6. **Find specific details**—facts. In this type of question you should be able to underline the answer. It will be there almost word for word.

Strategy

Read the stem first.
Read the passage, underlining words that pertain to the question. You need only a general idea of what you are looking for.
Read the question and the answer choices, eliminating the obviously wrong choices.
Refer to the passage to find the answer.

Example:

1 They came from almost every place and for almost every reason. They
2 came not because of gold, but golden tans. They came because they
3 would look better. Didn't the people in the commercials all look
4 terrific? They came because they wanted "the good life"—sun, sand

5 and youth. They came because you could do your own thing, whatever
6 that was. They came because it was the pot of gold at the end of
7 the rainbow. They came because it was California.

18. People came to California for all of the following reasons except

(A) to do what they wished
(B) the beach life
(C) hope of dreams fulfilled
(D) to stay young
(E) gold

Strategy. Read the stem of the question and underline *except*. When a question has *except*, you must be able to find the other four answer choices in the passage. You will have to check all of the choices. Sometimes exactly the same words are given in the question as in the passage; at other times synonyms are used.

In this case, read the answer choices first. As you read the passage, underline the words that might fit. Read the answer choices again. Locate the terms in the passage and start eliminating. This is an elimination-process question, unless you are certain that one of the answer choices is not in the passage.

(A) to do what they wished—"do your own thing," line 5
(B) beach life—"sun, sand," line 4
(C) hope of dreams fulfilled—"pot of gold at the end of the rainbow," lines 6 and 7.
(D) to stay young—"youth," line 5
(E) gold—"*not* because of gold," line 2. This is it! (Don't be misled by "pot of gold," line 6. That is a proverbial expression, not intended literally.)

7. **Analyze logic and order.** This type of question gives you a lot of data to sort out. Don't let it throw you. Organize and conquer. Take the time to draw a chart of the information on the question booklet, using your own shorthand. This type of question takes time. If there is only one such question *and* if you're short of time, guess and come back to it later. The chart gives you a particular advantage if there are several questions dealing with the same information, because your work is all done. All you need to do is read the information off the chart.

Example

39. The seventh grade is going on a two-day field trip. Each student's gear must include a sleeping bag, pup tent, backpack or ruck-sack and a poncho or a jacket with a rain hat. A sleeping bag with a rain cover may be used instead of a sleeping bag and pup tent.

Which of the following combinations of equipment is correct?

    I. sleeping bag with rain cover, jacket, rain hat

    II. sleeping bag, rucksack, jacket, rain hat

    III. sleeping bag, pup tent, backpack, poncho

(A) I only
(B) II only
(C) III only
(D) both II and III
(E) both I and III

Read the question. Make a chart.

	SB/RC	PT	BP/RS	P/J&RH	*Eliminate*
I.	✔			✔	no; A, E
II.	✔		✔	✔	no; B, D
III.	✔	✔	✔	✔	yes

Choice C is your answer.

8. **Fill in words omitted in a reading passage.** Some tests have a series of reading passages with about ten words omitted in each. You are to fill in each space with one of four choices of words. The passages are usually on educational topics.

Example:

It has been said that we can't have another 1. _____ because wealth, especially stocks, is no longer 2. _____ in a few hands, but spread among many. In times of 3. _____, when people could save money, they didn't, because prices were going up and credit was 4. _____ available. More and more people borrowed heavily, expecting to repay with cheaper money and sell at even more 5. _____ prices. People seem to expect everything to continue to go up and are always 6. _____ when prices fall. The old adage "What goes up, must come down" is still 7. _____. Had business, government and people saved money 8. _____ borrowing, they and the economy would be better off. It is strange that our 9. _____, which claims to encourage saving, taxes savings and allows deductions for interest payments, in essence 10. _____ borrowing.

  1. (A) war
     (B) famine
     (C) depression
     (D) inflation

2. (A) dispersed
   (B) concentrated
   (C) only
   (D) spread

3. (A) peace
   (B) wealth
   (C) war
   (D) inflation

4. (A) readily
   (B) not
   (C) somewhat
   (D) everywhere

5. (A) inflated
   (B) gross
   (C) deflated
   (D) difficult

6. (A) comforted
   (B) surprised
   (C) encouraged
   (D) depressed

7. (A) questionable
   (B) valid
   (C) trite
   (D) gospel

8. (A) in addition to
   (B) to increase
   (C) instead of
   (D) while

9. (A) government
   (B) population
   (C) president
   (D) bank

10. (A) decrying
    (B) taxing
    (C) defeating
    (D) subsidizing

Strategy

Fill your own word in first. Then, of the four choices, choose the word closest to your own word. Write the word in the space. Follow this procedure for the rest of the passage.

Read the passage with the filled-in words to see whether it makes sense.

Circle the words you used. Transfer your circled choices to the answer sheet.

Answers: 1. **C**   2. **B**   3. **D**   4. **A**   5. **A**   6. **B**   7. **B**   8. **C**   9. **A**   10. **D**

GRAMMAR REVIEW

Remember the basic rule: Choose the answer that "sounds" right to you.

Keep a secretarial handbook by your side, but not during the test. I use one all the time. It answers many grammar and usage questions concisely.

1. Be sure you know the correct use and spelling of **pronouns.**
   it, it's, its
   their, there, they're
   he and I, him and me

2. **Paired words** are "buddies." If you use one, you must use the other also: either . . . or; neither . . . nor; not only . . . but also.

3. The **subject and verb** in a sentence must **agree.** If the subject is singular, the verb must be singular.
   He (look, *looks*) sick.

4. The verb must be in the right **tense.**
   Yesterday I (*went*, gone) to school.

5. Correct **spelling** is a matter of looking words up, memorizing them and practicing them. Look words up in the dictionary if you aren't sure of their spelling. Write the word correctly ten times. (Remember fourth grade?) Repetition will help you memorize the word. Practice using the word in your writing.

6. Know when to **capitalize.** Titles: Generally, the only words not capitalized in titles are words of four or fewer letters that are articles, conjunctions or prepositions. A short word is capitalized if it is the first or last word of a title.
   He wrote *The Fall of Rome.*
Specific course titles are capitalized, as are courses named after countries or languages.
   I am taking History 102, English Composition 5, Mathematics II and Advanced Physics.
   I am studying American history, English, algebra and physics.
The first word of a quotation is capitalized.
   She exclaimed, "But I've just arrived!"
The first word of every line of poetry is capitalized.

7. **Use words correctly.** Some people are confused about the correct use and spelling of the following words. Check the dictionary for further information.

Accidentally. Note the second *a.*
Affect is most often used as a verb meaning "influence." *Effect* is sometimes used as a noun (as in "to have an *effect* on something") and sometimes as a verb meaning "to bring about."
All right, not *alright.*
Already means "previously." *All ready* means "all prepared."
Between two people or things, but *among* three or more people or things.
Use *number of* when something can be counted (cars) and *amount of* when it can't (flour).
Anxious means "worried," while *eager* means "looking forward" to something.
"*Bring* the book" means that the book will be moved toward the speaker. "*Take* the book" means that the book will be moved away from the speaker.
Use *farther* when discussing actual distance and *further* when meaning metaphorical distance.

He ran *farther* than I.

I have gone *further* in my profession than anyone else in my class.

Fewer is used with objects that can be counted, *less* with an amount that cannot ("fewer cars"; "less flour").

A speaker *implies* (suggests), while a listener *infers* (interprets).

Use *regardless,* not *irregardless.*

Latest means "most recent" while *last* means "after all others."

We had the *latest* news.

Harry came in *last* in the race.

To *raise* is to lift something else. To *rise* is to lift oneself.

The man who raises the profits will rise in the company as surely as the sun rises in the sky.

Scarcely and *hardly* do not take *not.*

To *set* is to place something. To *sit* is to seat oneself.

"Be sure *to* go," not "Be sure *and* go."

Perfect and *unique* do not need any strengthening adjectives. They represent the ultimate; words like *very* and *totally* are redundant with them.

"I would *have* gone," not "I would *of* gone."

8. **Synonyms** are words that have the same meaning.
   The new program caused *controversy*. A synonym for *controversy* is
   (A) *debate*   (B) anger   (C) comparison   (D) agreement

9. **Antonyms** are words that have opposite meanings.
   The antonym of *praise* is
   (A) laud   (B) *chide*   (C) detest   (D) emulate

10. Be able to recognize **similes** ("She looked *like* a rose." "He was as helpless *as* a child") and **metaphors** ("She *is* a rose").

11. You should be able to discern whether a sentence gives a **comparison, details, reason** or **explanation.**

12. Finding the **main idea** is discussed in the reading review.

MATHEMATICS REVIEW

The following are the types of math problems that you are most likely to have on the test. The distribution of problems on a particular test will vary. Check the sample test for the topics you need to cover. Not everything in the review is used on each test.

Type	Approximate Distribution
Word problems	20%
Equations	10–15%
Fractions	10%
Graphs	10%
Ratio and proportion	5–10%
Percentages	5%
Substitution in formulas	5%
Comparing and ordering numbers	5%
Estimation	5%
Measurement	5%
Logical reasoning	5–10%

TERMS

Perimeter—the distance around the edge of something.

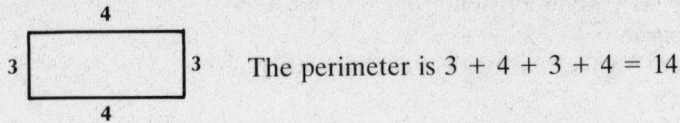

4

3   3   The perimeter is 3 + 4 + 3 + 4 = 14

4

Area—the size of the enclosed space. The area of the above rectangle is 3 × 4 = 12.

Prime number—a number that can be divided evenly only by itself and by 1, such as 2, 3, 5, 7.

Ratio—the comparison of two quantities. 10:13 or $^{10}/_{13}$

Proportion—two ratios equal to each other. $^{10}/_{13}$ = $^{20}/_{26}$

Counting numbers—1, 2, 3, 4 . . . .

Whole numbers—0, 1, 2, 3, 4 . . . .

Integers— . . . −4 −3, −2, −1, 0, 1, 2, 3, 4 . . .

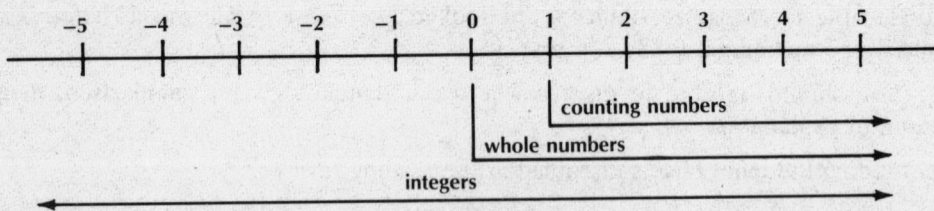

Factor—a number that divides evenly into another number.

3 × 4 = 12
3 and 4 are factors of 12

Square—the product of a number multiplied by itself.

The square of 5 is 25
5 × 5 = 25
Written: 5^2 = 25

Square root—a number that, when multiplied by itself, equals a given number.

The square root of 25 is 5
5 × 5 = 25
Written: $\sqrt{25}$ = 5

Cylinder—the shape of a tin can

Cube—a block whose length, width and height are all the same

NUMBER PLACEMENT

1	2	3	4	.	5	6	7	8
T	H	T	O	.	T	H	T	T
H	U	E	N	.	E	U	H	E
O	N	N	E	.	N	N	O	N
U	D	S	S	.	T	D	U	T
S	R				H	R	S	H
A	E				S	E	A	O
N	D					D	N	U
D	S					T	D	S
S						H	T	A
						S	H	N
							S	D
								T
								H
								S

					$\frac{5}{10}$	$\frac{6}{100}$	$\frac{7}{1,000}$	$\frac{8}{10,000}$
1,000	200	30	4					

To find what a number to the left of the decimal represents, put a 1 under the number and add zeros up to the decimal point.

$$1234.5678 \quad \text{so, } 2 \text{ represents two } hundreds$$
$$100.$$

To find out what a number to the right of the decimal represents, put a 1 below the decimal point and a zero for each place up to and including the place where the number is. Put a line and a 1 over the number.

$$1234.5678 = \frac{1}{1000} \quad \frac{1}{1,000} \quad \text{so, } 7 \text{ represents seven thousandths}$$

Hint: *-th* is for numbers *after* the decimal. They are parts of 1, that is, less than 1.

ROUNDING OFF

To round off, write the number you are rounding off to under the number. Your answer will have the same number of zeros. If the number above the first zero on the left is less than 5, leave the number on the left alone, and put zeros in the places to the right of the 1.

Round off to the nearest 1,000.

63,456.

1,000.

Write: 63,000

If the number above the first zero is 5 or more, add 1 to the number on the left and put zeros in the places to the right of the 1.

Round off to the nearest 1,000.

63,654

1,000

Write: 64,000

NUMBER LINE

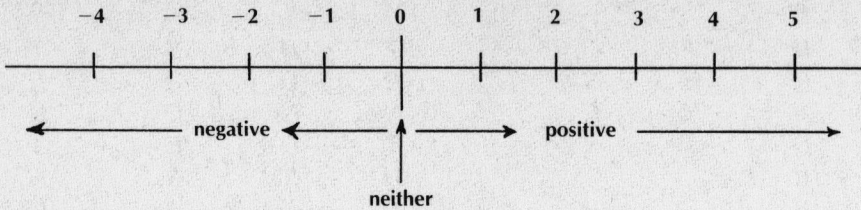

Example:

34. The fraction ¹²⁄₁₁ is between each of the following pairs of numbers except

    (A) ⅔ and ⁴⁄₃
    (B) ⁹⁄₁₁ and ¹¹⁄₉
    (C) 1 and 2
    (D) 0.9 and 1.1
    (E) ¹¹⁄₁₂ and ¹²⁄₁₂

Underline the word *except.*

Draw a number line.

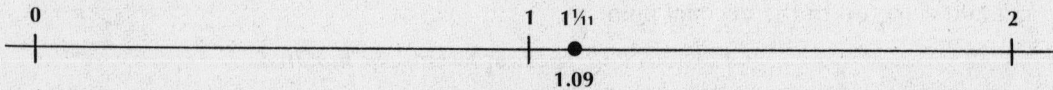

Change ¹²⁄₁₁ to 1 ¹⁄₁₁ (12 ÷ 11 = 1 ¹⁄₁₁). Change ¹²⁄₁₁ to a decimal: 12 ÷ 11 = 1.09
    Locate your results on the number line. Mark it with a dot. Write the fraction above the line and the decimal below the line. You're ready to compare ¹²⁄₁₁ (or 1 ¹⁄₁₁ or 1.09) with either fractions or decimals, instead of converting each pair.
    Locate each pair on the number line, putting fractions above the line and decimals below it. Connect each pair. Is the dot between each pair? The correct pair is the one that doesn't have the dot between them.

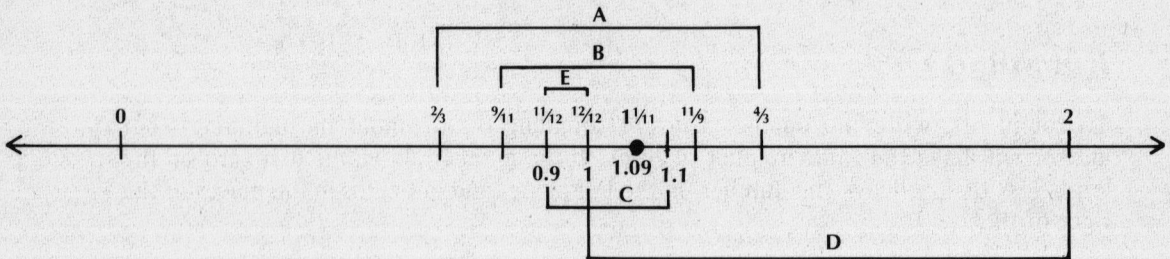

The correct answer is E.
    Another way to solve this problem is to compare fractions (see page 32). Decimals are changed to fractions.

$$\text{(A)} \quad \frac{\overset{22}{2}}{\underset{11}{3}} \diagdown \frac{\overset{36}{12}}{\underset{11}{}} \diagdown \frac{\overset{44}{4}}{\underset{3}{}} \qquad \text{36 is between 22 and 44.}$$

$$\text{(B)} \quad \frac{\overset{99}{9}}{11} \diagdown \frac{\overset{132/108}{12}}{11} \diagdown \frac{\overset{121}{11}}{9} \qquad \begin{array}{l} \text{132 is bigger than 99.} \\ \text{108 is smaller than 121.} \end{array}$$

(C)

11	12	22
$\frac{1}{1}$	$\frac{12}{11}$	$\frac{2}{1}$

12 is between 11 and 22.

(D)

99	120	121
$\frac{9}{10}$	$\frac{12}{11}$	$\frac{11}{10}$

120 is between 99 and 121.

(E)

121	144	132
$\frac{11}{12}$	$\frac{12}{11}$	$\frac{12}{12}$

144 is *not* between 121 and 132.

DIVISION

To check your answer, multiply the answer by the number you divided by. The result should be the number you started with.

$$12 \div 3 = 4$$
$$\text{Check: } 4 \times 3 = 12$$

To find out whether a number is divisible (can be divided evenly) by a certain number, remember:

A number is divisible by 2 if it ends in an even number: 2, 4, 6, 8.
A number is divisible by 3 if the digits add up to a number divisible by 3.

Is 1,542 divisible by 3?
Add the digits: $1 + 5 + 4 + 2 = 12$.
Is 12 divisible by 3? $12 \div 3 = 4$
Yes, 1,542 is divisible by 3.

A number is divisible by 5 if it ends in 0 or 5.
A number is divisible by 9 if the digits add up to a number divisible by 9.
A number is divisible by 10 if it ends in 0.

FRACTIONS

$$\frac{3}{5} = \frac{\text{numerator}}{\text{denominator}}$$

Adding fractions. To add fractions with the same denominator, simply add the numerators and repeat the denominator in the answer. Do *not* add the denominators.

$$\frac{1}{4} + \frac{2}{4} = \frac{3}{4}$$

To add fractions of unequal denominators, you must find the *common denominator* (CD for short) of these fractions. The CD is the number that all the denominators in the problem will divide into evenly.

$$\frac{1}{9} + \frac{2}{3}$$

Here, the CD is 9, since both 9 and 3 divide evenly into 9. One easy way to find the CD is to multiply the denominators by each other.

$$\frac{1}{2} + \frac{1}{3} \quad \text{The CD is } 2 \times 3 = 6$$

To add these two fractions, multiply both terms (numerator and denominator) of the first fraction by the denominator of the second fraction. Then multiply both terms of the second fraction by the denominator of the first fraction.

$$\frac{1 \times 3}{2 \times 3} + \frac{1 \times 2}{3 \times 2} =$$

$$\frac{3}{6} + \frac{2}{6} = \frac{5}{6}$$

Sometimes this system gets into large numbers that are unwieldy.

$$\frac{1}{8} + \frac{1}{12} - \frac{1}{15} \quad \text{The CD is } 8 \times 12 \times 15 = 1,440$$

Here we use the *lowest common denominator* (LCD), which is the smallest number that each denominator will divide into evenly.

Here's how. Divide the denominators by their factors. Start dividing by the smallest number that you can see will go evenly into at least one of the denominators. In this example, your first factor is 2. Continue with the same factor until you need to try a larger one. Factor until each denominator is down to 1.

Factor	Denominators			
	8	12	15	$8 \div 2 = 4, 12 \div 2 = 6$
2	4	6	15	Since 2 won't go evenly into 15,
2	2	3	15	just bring 15 down.
2	1	3	15	
3	1	1	5	
5	1	1	1	

Multiply the factors together to get the LCD: $2 \times 2 \times 2 \times 3 \times 5 = 120$

Now divide each denominator into the LCD. This is the number that you will multiply both the numerator and denominator of each fraction by.

$$120 \div 8 = 15$$
$$120 \div 12 = 10$$
$$120 \div 15 = 8$$

$$\frac{1 \times 15}{8 \times 15} + \frac{1 \times 10}{12 \times 10} - \frac{1 \times 8}{15 \times 8} =$$

$$\frac{15}{120} + \frac{10}{120} - \frac{8}{120}$$

$$\frac{15 + 10 - 8}{120} = \frac{17}{120}$$

Comparing fractions

Example:

16. Which is bigger, $\frac{4}{5}$ or $\frac{11}{13}$?

$$\text{Cross-multiply} \quad \overset{52}{}\underset{5}{\overset{4}{\diagdown}}\overset{55}{\underset{13}{\diagup}}\overset{11}{}$$

$$4 \times 13 = 52; \; 11 \times 5 = 55$$

55 is bigger than 52, therefore $\frac{11}{13}$ is bigger than $\frac{4}{5}$.

You can repeat this process for a question like the following.

Example:

23. Which fraction is smallest?

    (A) ⅔
    (B) ¾
    (C) 7⁄11
    (D) 9⁄10
    (E) 5⁄9

Underline *smallest.*

Compare $\overset{8}{}\underset{3}{\overset{2}{\diagdown}}\overset{9}{\underset{4}{\diagup}}\overset{3}{}$ ⅔ is smaller; cross out B (¾)

Compare $\overset{22}{}\underset{3}{\overset{2}{\diagdown}}\overset{21}{\underset{11}{\diagup}}\overset{7}{}$ 7⁄11 is smaller; cross out A (⅔)

Compare $\overset{70}{}\underset{11}{\overset{7}{\diagdown}}\overset{66}{\underset{10}{\diagup}}\overset{6}{}$ 9⁄10 is smaller; cross out C (7⁄11)

Compare $\overset{54}{}\underset{10}{\overset{6}{\diagdown}}\overset{50}{\underset{9}{\diagup}}\overset{5}{}$ 5⁄9 is smaller; cross out D (9⁄10)

E (5⁄9) is the answer.

Reducing fractions to their lowest terms. Divide the numerator and denominator by the same number until one number can't be divided any more. Start with the smallest or easiest numbers first, for example, 2, 3 or 10.

$$\frac{42 \div 2}{48 \div 2} = \frac{21}{24} \qquad \frac{21 \div 3}{24 \div 3} = \frac{7}{8}$$

or

$$\frac{\overset{7}{\cancel{\overset{21}{\cancel{42}}}}}{\underset{8}{\cancel{\underset{24}{\cancel{48}}}}} = \frac{7}{8}$$

Fraction, Decimal and Percent Equivalents

Memorize:

½ =	0.5 =	50%	⅚ =	0.83 =	83%
⅓ =	0.33 =	33%	⅐ =	0.14 =	14%
⅔ =	0.67 =	67%	⅛ =	0.125 =	12½%
¼ =	0.25 =	25%	⅜ =	0.375 =	37½%
¾ =	0.75 =	75%	⅝ =	0.625 =	62½%
⅕ =	0.2 =	20%	⅞ =	0.875 =	87½%
⅖ =	0.4 =	40%	⅑ =	0.11 =	11%
⅗ =	0.6 =	60%	⅒ =	0.1 =	10%
⅘ =	0.8 =	80%	1/11 =	0.09 =	9%
⅙ =	0.17 =	17%	1/12 =	0.08 =	8%

Memory aids:

⅐ = 0.14 (14 is double 7)

⅑ = 0.11   1/11 = 0.09

Fraction to decimal. To obtain the decimal equivalent of a fraction, divide the numerator by the denominator.

$$\frac{3}{4} = 4\overset{0.75}{\overline{)3.00}} = 0.75$$

Decimal to fraction. Put 1 and as many zeros as there are numbers to the right of the decimal in the denominator. Drop the decimal point and write the given number as the numerator. You have converted the decimal to a fraction. Now reduce the fraction to its lowest terms.

$$0.75 = \frac{75}{100} = \frac{3}{4}$$

Fraction to percent. Multiply the numerator by 100, divide by the denominator and add a percent sign.

$$\frac{3}{4} = \frac{3 \times 100}{4} = 75\%$$

Remember, *percent* means *part of 100.*

0.75 means 75 parts of 100, and is $\frac{75}{100}$

75% means 75 parts of 100, and is $\frac{75}{100}$

Percent to fraction. Put the number before the percent sign in the numerator and 100 in the denominator; reduce.

$$75\% = \frac{75}{100} = \frac{3}{4}$$

Decimal to percent. Move the decimal point two places to the right (in other words, multiply by 100). Add the percent sign.

$$.75 = .75_{\curvearrowright} = 75.\%$$
delete point: 75%

Percent to decimal. Move the decimal point two places to the left (in other words, divide by 100). Drop the percent sign.

$$75\% = .75._{\curvearrowleft} = .75$$

RATIO AND PROPORTION

Ratio is the comparison of two quantities. For instance, a quantity of 4 and a quantity of 20 compare on a ratio of 1 to 5 (1:5). The quantities 4 and 20 are written in fraction form as $\frac{4}{20}$ or in ratio form as 4:20 and, when reduced, become $\frac{1}{5}$ or 1:5 (in this instance, the result of dividing both the numerator and the denominator by 4). Therefore, 4 compares with 20 the same as 1 compares with 5. They compare on a *ratio* of 1 to 5 or 1:5.

Example:

6. Which pair of numbers has a ratio of 4 to 9?

   (A) 49 and 94
   (B) 18 and 23
   (C) 63 and 28
   (D) 28 and 63
   (E) 94 and 49

In numbers having a ratio of 4 to 9, the first number is divisible by 4 and the second by 9. When you divide the first number by 4 and the second by 9, the answers should be the same. The order of numbers is important. Here the smaller number is first. 4 is less than 9. 4 to 9 is not the same as 9 to 4. Are 8 and 18 in a ratio of 4 to 9?

$$8 \div 4 = 2 \quad \text{and} \quad 18 \div 9 = 2$$

$$or \quad \frac{8 \div 4 = 2}{18 \div 9 = 2} \quad or \quad \frac{8 \div 2 = 4}{18 \div 2 = 9}$$

Strategy.

Eliminate choices in which the numbers are in the wrong order, as in C and E, above. Now look at the remaining choices.

   (A) 49 cannot be divided evenly by 4
   (B) 18 cannot be divided evenly by 4
   (D) 28 can be divided evenly by 4: $28 \div 4 = 7$
       63 can be divided evenly by 9: $63 \div 9 = 7$

   (D) is the answer. Check: $\frac{28}{63} = \frac{4}{9}$

Example:

47. On an assignment, a pupil did 15 problems correctly and 6 problems incorrectly. What is the ratio of correct to incorrect problems?

Strategy.

Underline *correct* and *incorrect*.

$$\text{ratio is } \frac{\text{correct}}{\text{incorrect}} = \frac{15}{6}_{\text{(reduce)}} = \frac{5}{2} \text{ or 5 to 2 or 5:2}$$

Example:

48. The scale of a drawing is 1:36. This means that

    (A) 1 in. = 36 ft
    (B) 3 ft = 6 yd
    (C) 1 ft = 3 yd
    (D) 1 ft = 12 yd
    (E) 1 ft = 3 ft

To compare, you must use the same unit of measurement. Change each to the same measurement, and you will have

    (A) 1 in. = 432 in.
    (B) 3 ft = 18 ft
    (C) 1 ft = 9 ft
    (D) 1 ft = 36 ft
    (E) 1 ft = 3 ft

The answer is clearly D.

A *proportion* is two ratios with an equal sign between them.

$$\frac{5}{6} = \frac{10}{12} \text{ or } 5:6 = 10:12 \text{ or } 5:6::10:12$$

Example:

33. At the rate of 5 items for 24¢, how many items can you get for 96¢?

$$\frac{24¢}{96¢} = \frac{5 \text{ items}}{i \text{ items}} \qquad 24i = 5 \times 96 \qquad i = \frac{5 \times 96}{24} = 20$$

Example:

20. To get a C on her next test, Susan needs at least 70%, which is 91 questions correct. How many questions are there on the test?

$$\frac{\text{part}}{\text{whole}} = \frac{\text{part}}{\text{whole}} \qquad \frac{70\%}{100\%} = \frac{91 \text{ questions}}{\text{total questions}} \qquad \frac{70}{100} = \frac{91}{x}$$

Cross multiply $70x = 91 \times 100$

Divide by 70 $\quad \dfrac{70x}{70} = \dfrac{91 \times 100}{70}$

$$x = 130 \text{ questions.}$$

Don't multiply too soon, because often you can cancel to get the correct answer.

$$\frac{\overset{13}{\cancel{91}} \times \cancel{100}}{\cancel{70}} = 130$$
$$1$$

When you are asked, "What part of something is something else?" just remember "is over of" $\left(\frac{\text{is}}{\text{of}}\right)$ and you won't get confused.

What part <u>of 6</u> <u>is 4</u>? $\quad \frac{\text{is}}{\text{of}} \quad \frac{4}{6} = \frac{2}{3}$

<u>4 is</u> what part <u>of 6</u>? $\quad \frac{\text{is}}{\text{of}} \quad \frac{4}{6} = \frac{2}{3}$

<u>15 is</u> what % <u>of 20</u>? To find percent (part of 100), just multiply by 100.

$$\frac{\text{is}}{\text{of}} \quad \frac{15}{20} \times 100 = 75\%$$

<u>28% of</u> what number <u>is 70</u>? Estimate 28% is close to 25% or ¼. You want the total number (100%), so the answer will be about $4 \times 70 = 280$.

$$\frac{\text{is}}{\text{of}} \quad \frac{70 \times 100}{28} = 250$$

FACTORS

Factors are numbers that, multiplied together, make up a given number.

$$2 \times 3 \times 4 = 24$$
$$\uparrow \quad \uparrow \quad \nearrow$$
$$\text{factors}$$

Another way of saying this is that a factor is a number that will divide evenly into a given number.

Factors of 12 are 2, 3, 4, 6

A *prime number* is a number that is divisible only by itself and 1. 0 and 1 are not primes. The primes are 2, 3, 5, 7, 11, 13, 17, 19, 23, 29. . . .

A *prime factor* is a factor that is prime. The prime factors of 12 are 2 and 3 ($4 = 2 \times 2$; $6 = 2 \times 3$). To find the prime factors of a number, divide by prime numbers until the number is completely factored. Start with easy numbers.

Example:

$$
\begin{array}{ll}
2 & 12 \\
2 & 6 \\
3 & 3 \\
\hline
1 & \quad 2 \times 2 \times 3 = 12
\end{array}
$$

Use the indicators of divisibility on page 31.

Example:

15. What is the smallest prime factor of 1,683?

    (A) 0
    (B) 1
    (C) 2
    (D) 3
    (E) 11

Strategy. Underline *smallest* prime. 0 and 1 are not primes, so cross out (A) and (B). The number is not even, so it can't be divided by 2; therefore cross out (C). To find out whether 1,683 is divisible by 3, add the digits: $1 + 6 + 8 + 3 = 18$. Divide by 3. $18 \div 3 = 6$. D is the answer. You don't need even to try (E) since you have your answer in (D). If you divide 1,683 by 11, you'll find it is a factor, but it isn't the *smallest* prime factor.

SQUARES AND SQUARE ROOTS

The *square* of a number is the number multiplied by itself.

$$\text{the square of } 9 = 9 \times 9 = 9^2 = 81$$

The *square root* of a number is the opposite of the square; it is the number which multiplied by itself produces the square. The square root of 9 is

$$\sqrt{9} = \sqrt{3 \times 3} = \sqrt{3^2} = 3$$

Memorize:

Squares	Square Roots
$1^2 = 1$	$\sqrt{1} = 1$
$2^2 = 4$	$\sqrt{4} = 2$
$3^2 = 9$	$\sqrt{9} = 3$
$4^2 = 16$	$\sqrt{16} = 4$
$5^2 = 25$	$\sqrt{25} = 5$
$6^2 = 36$	$\sqrt{36} = 6$
$7^2 = 49$	$\sqrt{49} = 7$
$8^2 = 64$	$\sqrt{64} = 8$
$9^2 = 81$	$\sqrt{81} = 9$
$10^2 = 100$	$\sqrt{100} = 10$
$11^2 = 121$	$\sqrt{121} = 11$
$12^2 = 144$	$\sqrt{144} = 12$

Estimating square roots. For every two digits under the square root sign there is one digit in the answer. To determine the number of digits in the answer, underline groups of two digits, moving left from the imaginary decimal. If there are an odd number of digits, count one place for the extra digit.

$$\sqrt{\underline{12}\ \underline{34}} \qquad\qquad \sqrt{\underline{1}\ \underline{23}\ \underline{45}}$$

Estimate: Two places in the answer

$\sqrt{12}$ is between $\sqrt{9} = 3$ and $\sqrt{16} = 4$
Answer is between 30 and 40.
    $30^2 = 900$ and $40^2 = 1,600$
1200 is closer to 900 than 1,600, so try 33.

Three places in the answer

$\sqrt{1} = 1$
Answer is between 100 and 200
    $100^2 = 10,000$ and $200^2 = 40,000$
Answer is closer to 100.

$$33 \times 33 = 1089 \text{ too small}$$
$$35 \times 35 = 1225 \text{ closest}$$

$$110 \times 110 = 12,100 \text{ too small}$$
$$115 \times 115 = 13,225 \text{ too big}$$
$$113 \times 113 = 12,769 \text{ too big}$$
$$111 \times 111 = 12,321 \text{ closest}$$

AVERAGES

An average is the sum of a group of items divided by the number of items.

The average of 7, 11, 13 and 19 is
$$\frac{7 + 11 + 13 + 19}{4} = \frac{40}{4} = 10$$
(4 numbers)

Example:

11. John tries to average 5 miles a day. He ran 4 miles on Monday and Wednesday, 3 on Tuesday, 5 on Thursday, 6 on Friday and 8 on Saturday. How many miles will he have to run on Sunday to make his goal?

To average 5 miles a day, he needs to run a total of $5 \times 7 = 35$ miles. The total for Monday through Saturday is $4 + 4 + 3 + 5 + 6 + 8 = 30$. He needs to run 5 miles on Sunday. $(35 - 30 = 5)$

BASIC UNITS OF MEASURE

	Avoirdupois		**Metric**
When we use	pound (lb)	others use	kilogram (kg)
	ounce (oz)		gram (g)
	foot (ft) or yard (yd)		meter (m)
	inch (in.)		centimeter (cm)
	gallon (gal) quart (qt)		liter (l)
	mile (mi)		kilometer (km)

Approximate Equivalents

1 meter	=	1 yd plus
2½ cm	=	1 in.
1 kg	=	2 lb plus
30 g	=	1 oz
1 liter	=	1 qt
1 km	=	½ mi plus

Temperature

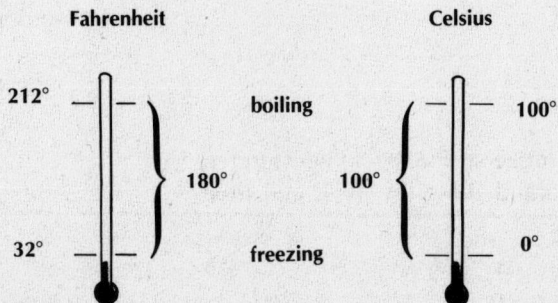

Conversion formula: $\frac{5}{9}(F-32) = C$ $\frac{9}{5}C + 32 = F$

Approximation: $\frac{F-30}{2} \approx C$ $2C + 30 \approx F$

WORD PROBLEMS

Do you shudder at the thought of word problems? The key is that they are translation problems. You need to translate from English to the international language of mathematics. Mathematics is a language like music, chemistry and physics; symbols replace words. Underline the key facts and what you want to know.

Example:

25. The cost of a cabin rental is $20 per night plus $5 for each person. How much will it cost Adele and her seven friends to stay three nights?

base cost @ night $20
number of people 8
cost per person $5
number of nights 3

(base cost + per person) × (number of nights) = total cost
($20 + 5 × 8) × (3) =
($20 + 40) × (3) =
$60 × 3 = $180

Example:

40. A total of 2,315 football fans will be traveling to a game in buses. Each bus can carry 50 passengers. How many buses will be needed?

$$\frac{\text{number of people}}{\text{number in each bus}} = \text{number of buses}$$

$$\frac{2315}{50} = 46\frac{15}{50} \text{ buses}$$

Can you hire $\frac{15}{50}$ of a bus? No. You need 1 more bus for a total of 47 buses.

Always check an answer to see that it makes sense. When there are large numbers, substitute small ones to get the formula. Try to make the answer you're looking for the unknown.

Discounts

Example:

37. What is the price of a $50.00 chair after it has been marked down by 10% and then 20%?

(A) $45.00
(B) $36.00
(C) $35.00

(D) $9.00
(E) $4.00

Long way:

$50.00 × 0.10 = $5.00
$50.00–$5.00 = $45.00
$45.00 × 0.20 = $9.00
$45.00 − $9.00 = $36.00

Short way:

$50.00 × 0.90 = $45.00
$45.00 × 0.80 = $36.00

Note: It is not 30% off, because you take 20% off the $45.00, not off the $50.00.

Age

Example:

18. Louisa is four years older than Gilbert.
Eight years ago she was twice as old as he.
How old is Louisa?

(A) 24
(B) 16
(C) 12
(D) 8
(E) 4

Strategy. You want to find Louisa's age now.

Ages now are L, G
Ages 8 years ago are $L - 8, G - 8$
Your two equations are:
$L = G + 4$
$L - 8 = 2(G - 8)$

You want to find L, so try to get rid of G.

$$L = G + 4$$

Subtract 4

$$-4 = -4$$

Use this in place of G.
Substitute
Now solve for L.

$$L - 4 = G$$
$$L - 8 = 2(L - 4 - 8)$$
$$L - 8 = 2(L - 12) \qquad \text{Tidy up}$$
$$L - 8 = 2L - 24$$
$$-L \qquad -L \qquad \text{get L on one side only}$$
$$-8 = L - 24 \qquad \text{get L all alone on one side}$$
$$+24 = +24$$
$$16 = L$$

Check

$$16 = G + 4$$
$$12 = G$$
$$16 - 8 = 2(12 - 8)$$
$$8 = 2 \times 4$$

This looks long, and you may take some short cuts, but you *can* solve it. You can also substitute the answers given, and see whether they work:

(A) 24   (B) 16   (C) 12   (D) 8   (E) 4

Substitute choice A: $L = 24, G = 20$ $24 - 8 \overset{?}{=} 2(20 - 8)$
$16 \overset{?}{=} 2 \times 12$ No.

Substitute choice B: $L = 16, G = 12$ $16 - 8 \overset{?}{=} 2(12 - 8)$
$8 \overset{?}{=} 2 \times 4$ Yes.

Try another problem, using the choices provided.

Example:

2. The difference between a two-digit number and the numbers reversed is 27. The sum of the digits is 7. What is the number?

    (A) 18
    (B) 43
    (C) 52
    (D) 61
    (E) 70

Strategy. What are they looking for? Numbers like 61 and 16. The number must meet two criteria. Check the easiest part first: do the digits add up to 7? 8 + 1 = 9; eliminate A. The others are still in the game. Check to see whether the difference is 27. Subtract the reversed numbers.

(B) 43	(C) 52	(D) 61	(E) 70
−34	−25	−16	− 7
9	27 Bingo!	45	63

You can eliminate some without subtraction, because an estimate will show you that the difference isn't close to 27.

GRAPHS

Read the information carefully. Use your pencil as a ruler to read the chart. Use the answer sheet as a straight-edge to draw grid lines, if necessary.

FORMULAS

$$\text{Interest} = \text{Principal} \times \text{Rate} \times \text{Time}$$
$$I = PRT$$
$$\text{Total amount to be repaid} = P + I \text{ (Principal and Interest)}$$
$$\text{Distance} = \text{Rate} \times \text{Time}$$
$$D = RT$$

GEOMETRY

Perimeter is distance around, such as fencing or fringe on a tablecloth.

Draw a rough diagram.

$$P = 2L + 2w \text{ } or \text{ } 2(L + w)$$

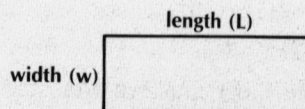

If you are unsure, substitute small numbers.

L = 3 $2 \times 3 + 2 \times 2 = 6 + 4 = 10$
w = 2

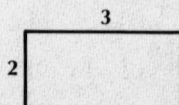

Area is the total space within a two-dimensional figure. The area of a rectangle = length × width: A = L × W. In the diagram on page 42, the area is 2 × 3 = 6.

Volume is the total space contained within a three-dimensional figure.

The volume of a rectangular solid
is length × width × height.

L = 6 in.
w = 4 in.
h = 5 in.

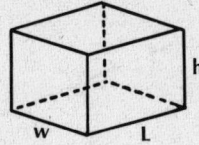

$$V = L \times w \times h$$
$$= 6 \times 4 \times 5$$
$$= 120 \text{ cubic inches}$$

Area of triangles

Area = ½h × b

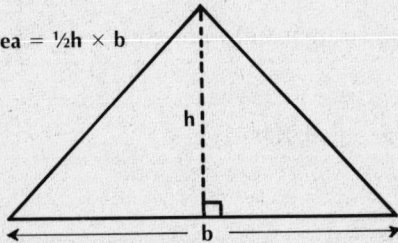

Area = ½ × 8 × 10 = 4 × 10 = 40

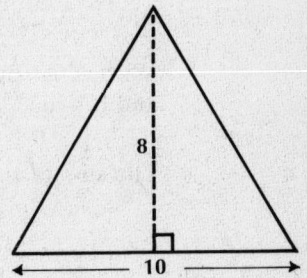

Area of rectangles

A = h × b

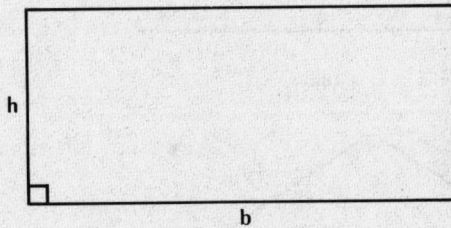

Area of parallelograms

A = h × b

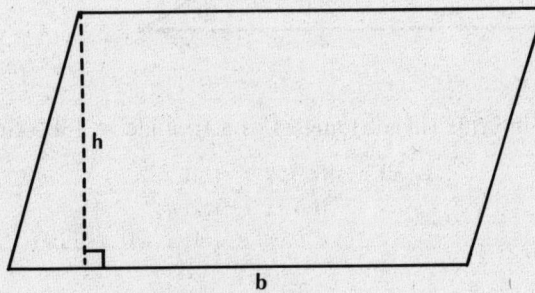

Circles

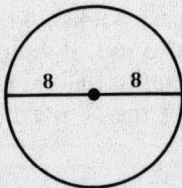

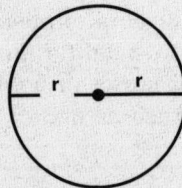

Radius: from center of circle to edge = r (8)
Diameter: from one edge through the center to the other edge d = 2r (16)
$\pi = 3.14$ or $\frac{22}{7}$
Area = $\pi r^2 = \pi(8)^2 = 64\pi$
Circumference = $2\,\pi\,r = 2\,\pi\,(8) = 16\,\pi$

Angles

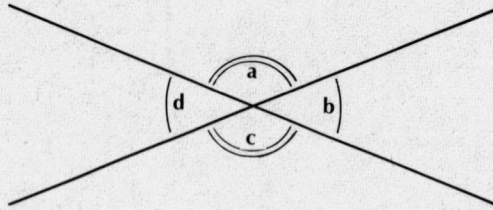

Vertical or opposite angles formed by intersecting straight lines are equal, so a = c, and b = d.

The sum of the angles on one side of a straight line equal 180°

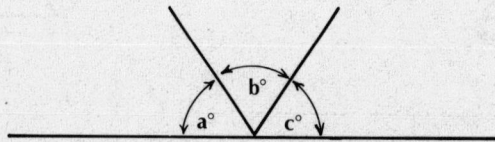

$$a + b + c = 180°$$

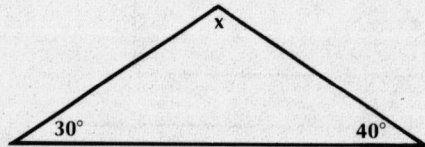

The sum of the interior (inside) angles of a triangle = 180°. So, to find x:

$$30 + 40 + x = 180°$$
$$70 + x = 180$$
$$x = 180 - 70 = 110°$$

ALGEBRA

Don't be thrown by the word algebra. Instead of using horses, books and people, algebra uses a, b, c . . . x, y, z to stand for anything you want to use. It's shorthand. You can then plug in numbers or horses or books or people. Caution! Do not confuse the x that represents an item, such as one of the horses, with the × that indicates multiplication.

Addition

$$7a^2 + 3a + 2a^2 = ?$$

You *can* add $7a^2 + 2a^2$ to get $9a^2$. Think: 7 horses + 2 horses = 9 horses. Add the numbers in front of the a^2s (or horses). These numbers are called the *coefficients*. Do not add the *exponents* (powers).

$$7a^2 + 2a^2 = (7 + 2)a^2 = 9a^2$$

(*not* $9a^4$; that is multiplying.) You *cannot* add a^2 and a. They are different animals.

$$7a^2 + 3a + 2a^2 = 9a^2 + 3a$$

Example:

17.   Find the perimeter

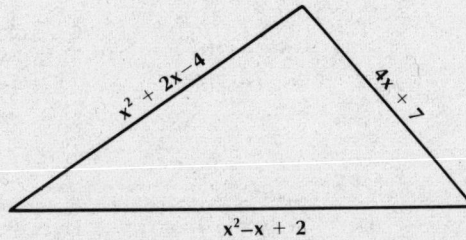

(triangle with sides labeled $x^2 + 2x - 4$, $4x + 7$, and $x^2 - x + 2$)

Perimeter is distance around. Add the sides up by first lining the figures up. Put x^2 under x^2 and x under x.

$$
\begin{array}{r}
x^2 + 2x - 4 \\
4x + 7 \\
x^2 - x + 2 \\
\hline
2x^2 + 5x + 5
\end{array}
$$
          Add each column

Add the numbers. If there is no number in front of an x or x^2, it is 1.

Subtraction. Remember that if there is a minus sign in front of a bracket and the bracket is removed, the sign of every term inside the bracket is changed.

$$3b^2 - 4b + c - (3b^2 + b - c) =$$
                                   this is positive
$$3b^2 - 4b + c - 3b^2 - b + c =$$

Now add up. $3b^2 - 3b^2 - 4b - b + c + c =$
          0          $-5b$ + $2c$ $= 2c - 5b$

Multiplication. A dot (·) is used to indicate multiplication, as well as × and nothing (as in 3a). Get your terms straight.

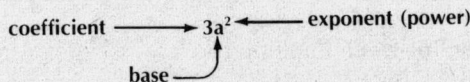

coefficient ⟶ $3a^2$ ⟵ exponent (power)

base ⟶

Add the exponents (powers) if the base is the same.

$$a \times a = a^1 \times a^1 = a^{1+1} = a^2$$

$$a^2 \times a^4 = a^{(2+4)} = a^6$$

$$a^2 \times b^3 = a^2b^3$$

Multiply the coefficients.

$$2a^2 \times 3a^3 = (2 \times 3)a^{(2+3)} = 6a^5$$

$$4a^2 \cdot 5b^3 = 20a^2b^3$$

When a term, such as $7a^2$, is followed by terms in brackets, multiply it by each term inside the brackets.

$$7a^2(a^2 - 2a + 3) =$$
$$7a^2 \cdot a^2 - 7a^2 \cdot 2a + 7a^2 \cdot 3 =$$
$$7a^4 - 14a^3 + 21a^2$$

Try $(x + 5)(x - 4) =$ or $x + 5$
$x(x - 4) + 5(x - 4) =$ $x - 4$
$x^2 - 4x + 5x - 20 =$ $\overline{x^2 + 5x}$
$x^2 + x - 20$ $-4x - 20$
                         $\overline{x^2 + x - 20}$

or

$(x + 5)(x - 4) = \quad x^2 + x - 20$

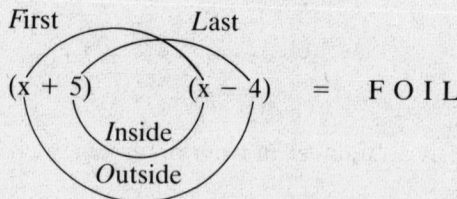

First   Last

$(x + 5) \qquad (x - 4) \qquad = \qquad$ F O I L

Inside

Outside

Solving Equations

Problem: Solve for x. $7x - 4 = 38$
Add 4 $+ 4 = + 4$
                 $\overline{}$
                 $\dfrac{7x}{7} \quad = \quad \dfrac{42}{7}$
Divide by 7
Solution: $x = 6$

You can also plug in the answer choices for x and see which one fits.

Problem: Find c. $b = 3c$

$$340 + 3b + c - 120 = 280$$

You want to find c, so substitute 3c for b, eliminating b.

                $340 + 3(3c) + c - 120 = 280$
Clean up $340 + 9c + c - 120 = 280$
Add like terms $340 - 120 + 10c = 280$
                $220 + 10c = 280$
Subtract 220 $\underline{-220 \qquad\qquad -220}$
Divide by 10 $10c = 60$
Solution: $c = 6$

When you multiply two or more numbers together and get a product of 0, at least one of those numbers must be 0. The product of any number and zero is always zero.

$$(12)(6)(7)(4)(3)(0) = 0$$

Problem: Solve for x.

$$x(x + 4) = 0$$

Either $x = 0$ or $x + 4 = 0$

If $x + 4 = 0$,

$$\frac{-4 = -4}{\text{then } x \quad = -4}$$

Solution: $x = 0$, $x = -4$ (one or the other or both)

To solve the following type of problem, set each factor equal to 0 and solve.

$$(x + 3)(x - 5) = 0$$
$$x + 3 = 0 \qquad x - 5 = 0$$
$$x = -3 \qquad x = 5$$

Coordinates

Y - distance up or down
X - distance right or left

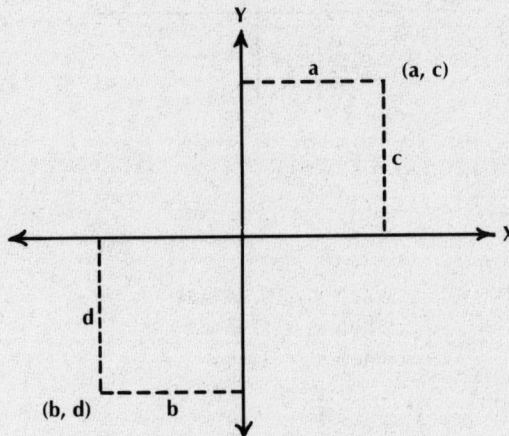

a is to the *right*, so it is positive (X)
b is to the *left*, so it is negative (X)
c is *up*, so it is *positive* (Y)
d is *down*, so it is *negative* (Y)

In general:

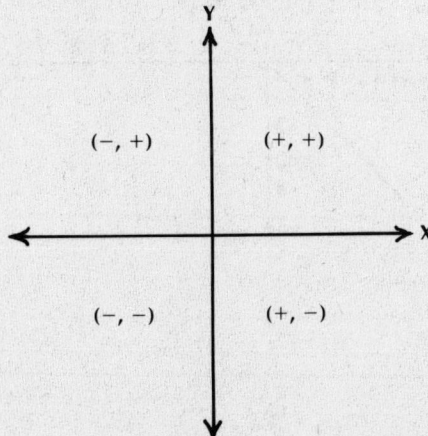

To plot (draw or graph) these equations, plug numbers in.

$$x = 2$$
$$y = -3$$

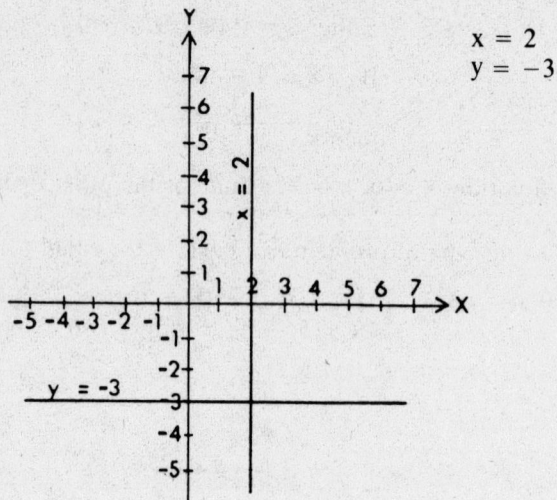

$$x = y$$
when $x = 0$, $y = 0$
when $x = 1$, $y = 1$
when $x = 2$, $y = 2$

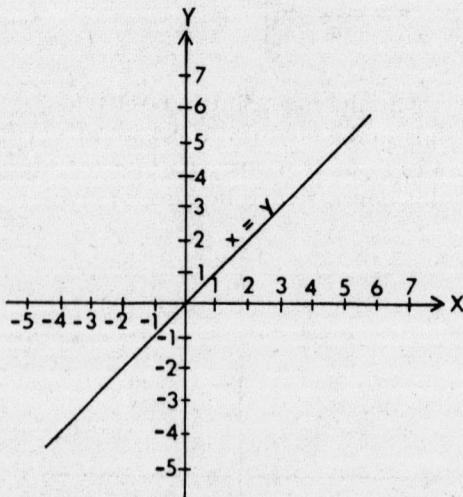

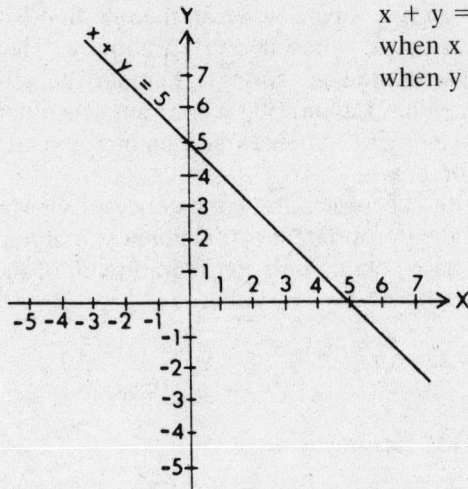

$$x + y = 5$$

when $x = 0$,	$0 + y = 5$	$y = 5$
when $y = 0$,	$x + 0 = 5$	$x = 5$

- If the equation has only x in it (no y), then the graph is a vertical line.
- If the equation has only y in it (no x), then the graph is a horizontal line.
- If x is 0 when y is 0, then the line passes through the origin, the point at which the x and y axes (lines) intersect (cross).

Use common sense (logic) on graphs. Substitute numbers. Eliminate the answers that don't fit.

WRITING REVIEW

The writing portion of the teacher's competency test is designed to measure your mastery of English and your ability to express your ideas clearly in written form. Neither your knowledge about a topic nor your viewpoint is a factor in the scoring. The topic is only a means of determining your ability to express yourself in standard English.

There are usually two types of topic in each test. With one type you are asked to express your thoughts about a remembered experience. With the other you are asked to take a position on a subject and defend it. In both instances you will need to marshal your thoughts so that you have 1) a topic sentence, 2) subpoints that support or expand on your theme and 3) a conclusion.

When the instructions for the topic ask you to include specific considerations or supporting arguments, be sure that you include them all. Support your generalizations with specifics. Stay within the guidelines of the topic, and don't write more than the space allows. You may write less. Length is not the criterion, but you should fill at least half the space given.

You may want to pattern your essays on the basic five-paragraph style. The first paragraph states the thesis and makes brief mention of the supporting statements; the next three paragraphs expand on the three main supporting statements; the last paragraph restates the thesis in other words and wraps it all up.

Strategy. For each topic, spend a third of your time jotting down your ideas, putting them in order and making an outline. Take half of the time to write the essay. This will leave you a few minutes to reread the essay(s) carefully, correcting mechanical errors. When you have to write on two topics, write on the one that is easiest for you first. If you have enough time, improve phrasing and vocabulary. The mechanics of written English are a major consideration in scoring: grammar, punctuation, sentence structure, vocabulary, paragraphing. Capitalizing school subjects other than languages, writing & for *and,* using incomplete sentences and ending a sentence with *and etc.* are some of the most common errors.

As you write and edit, keep in mind consistency of viewpoint, supporting arguments, organization, logic, appropriateness to audience, unity and cohesiveness. Scoring is done on a holistic basis, taking into consideration all of these points.

PRACTICE TOPICS

Here are topics you can use for practice.

What event in your life affected you most profoundly? Relate how it changed you and explain why the change was for the better or worse.

"A teacher has not taught until the student has learned." In which situations would you agree with this statement and under what circumstances would you disagree?

Which class in college has been of most benefit to you? Why?

Compare the practice of student teaching two periods a day for a year with student teaching all day for nine weeks. Which do you think is better? Support your opinions.

At some time in our lives we must face a situation about which we can do nothing. Relate such an incident, including how you dealt with it, your feelings at the time and its aftereffects on you.

Education is not an accumulation of facts, but the confidence of knowing that one can locate the facts when they are needed. Give reasons why you agree or disagree with this statement.

There are people who have greatly influenced our lives without knowing it. They could be famous people or people we have met only casually or even people we have never met. Describe the influence one such person has had on your life.

Do you think graded report cards in elementary school are beneficial or harmful to the students?

Which college class was most disappointing to you? If you were to teach that class, what changes would you make in it to improve it for the students?

It has been suggested that education professors and school district administrators teach an elementary or secondary school class every seventh year. Do you think this is a beneficial and workable idea or not?

What do you consider the most important character trait of a good teacher?

"Good teachers do not necessarily make good administrators." What is your opinion of this statement? Illustrate with examples from your experience, if possible.

PROFESSIONAL-KNOWLEDGE REVIEW

Some tests ask factual questions: "Do you know this?" Other tests ask application questions: "Johnny has been absent five days. From other students you hear that he has been at the playground these days. What would you do?" All questions are designed to test your knowledge of teaching concepts, theory and educational law.

The tests are based on the following topics, which you should be familiar with:

CLASSROOM MANAGEMENT

Managing students effectively
Disciplining students appropriately
Promoting student motivation
Individualizing the pace of instruction
Using a lesson plan effectively
Understanding the principles of group process; involving students in decision-making
Using time management in planning
Communicating effectively
Making use of the cultural diversity of students

CURRICULUM AND INSTRUCTION

Knowing and using goals and objectives
Developing the curriculum
Planning lessons
Selecting appropriate resources
Mainstreaming

EVALUATION

Knowing testing terminology
Differentiating between evaluation and assessment
Developing tests
Choosing the appropriate test
Administering tests
Interpreting tests
Grading tests fairly
Reporting student performance to parents or administrators
Utilizing test results to improve student performance

GROWTH AND LEARNING THEORIES

Identifying abnormal behavior for referral
Knowing the basic theories of child development and learning
Recognizing the common characteristics of various levels of physical, mental, social and emotional development
Understanding theories of motivation

EDUCATIONAL FOUNDATIONS

Recognizing the major issues in American education
Identifying major educational theorists and their contributions
Appreciating the effect of culture on education; creating techniques for accommodating the variety of cultures
Maintaining professional skills with the appropriate resources
Understanding the major purposes of public education in America

ADMINISTRATION AND ORGANIZATION

Knowing the various responsibilities and roles in education at the federal, state and local levels
Following nondiscriminatory practices
Understanding state law as it applies to education
Undertaking the legal responsibilities of teachers
Implementing policies on the promotion of students
Recognizing revenue sources for education
Knowing the major legal rulings affecting education
Cooperating with coworkers and parents
Realizing teachers', parents' and students' rights and responsibilities
Holding effective parent-teacher conferences
Engaging in effective communication with the public

You may have to study the particular state educational law to prepare for the tests in some states.

READING
60 Minutes–50 Questions

Directions: Choose the best answer for each question and blacken the corresponding space on the Answer Sheet for Sample Test 1. The correct answers and explanations follow the test.

Questions 1 and 2

A campaign to control malaria by spraying insecticides in remote mountain villages of Malaysia had an unexpected series of consequences. The insecticide not only killed the mosquitoes but also poisoned the cockroaches upon which the village cats fed. The cats died, and as a result, disease-bearing rats, whose population had previously been controlled by the cats, invaded the village. This chain reaction of problems was halted when a fresh supply of cats was sent to the village.

1. The central idea in the above passage is that

   (A) cats are important
   (B) there are worse things than malaria
   (C) insecticides can have harmful effects
   (D) acts have far-reaching effects
   (E) the food chain is precarious

2. Malaria is spread by

   (A) mosquitoes
   (B) cockroaches
   (C) cats
   (D) rats
   (E) villagers

Questions 3 and 4

As in many other cities, transportation in and out of San Francisco was designed according to the tenet that commuters would travel from the suburbs to work in the city. The decentralization of industry, especially high technology, has moved industry to the people who live in the suburbs. Now we see the phenomenon of city dwellers commuting to the suburbs to work.

3. One effect that can be expected from the development cited in the passage is:

   (A) Industries in the suburbs will move back to the city.
   (B) There will be more jobs in San Francisco.
   (C) People will spend more time commuting.
   (D) Road signs designating commuter traffic hours and directions will have to be changed.
   (E) There will be an increase in the number of people moving into San Francisco.

4. In this passage *tenet* means

   (A) faith
   (B) doctrine
   (C) belief
   (D) dogma
   (E) hold

5. "It would be civil of you to keep quiet about the incident," advised his fellow teacher. The meaning of *civil* in the above sentence is

   (A) polite
   (B) wise
   (C) nonmilitary
   (D) righteous
   (E) good citizenship

6. This past winter pilots reported changes in the mighty jet stream, the "rivers" of wind in the upper atmosphere. The weather has deviated considerably from normal: severe snow storms, thunderstorms, tornadoes in unlikely places, exceptionally cold weather, greater amounts of snow and rainfall than usual.

One can conclude that

   (A) the weather affects the jet stream
   (B) the jet stream affects the weather
   (C) there will be no more unusual weather
   (D) the weather will return to normal shortly
   (E) it will be an unusually hot summer

Questions 7 and 8

Amateur archeologists have unearthed a number of skeletons from a wheat field in Loudon County, Virginia. The oldest dates back to about 1200 B.C. This is about 2,800 years before the first European settlers arrived in Virginia. Artifacts found there date back to about 3500 B.C.

7. Approximately how many years old is the oldest skeleton?

    (A) 1,200
    (B) 2,800
    (C) 3,200
    (D) 3,500
    (E) 5,500

8. When did the first European settlers come to Virginia?

    (A) 1200 B.C.
    (B) 1200 A.D.
    (C) 3500 B.C.
    (D) 2800 B.C.
    (E) 1600 A.D.

9. After members of the Japanese Alpine Club reached the top of Mount Everest, Y. Muira, one of Japan's foremost skiers, skied nearly two miles down a 70° slope. High winds buffeted him, and during the run he fell, losing his right ski. He skied the rest of the distance on one ski, terminating his run just short of a crevasse.

    Muira did not continue his run because

    (A) he was at the bottom of the mountain
    (B) it was too windy
    (C) he couldn't continue skiing on one ski
    (D) it was too difficult to breathe at that altitude
    (E) there was a deep crack in the ice

Questions 10 and 11

We think of musicals as pure entertainment, but some have explored social issues that were not generally discussed at the time. The messages were slipped in amongst the singing and dancing. For example, *Showboat* and *South Pacific* both addressed racial prejudice. In *South Pacific* there were parallel stories, each emphasizing a certain aspect of racial prejudice.

10. The above passage

    (A) is racially prejudiced
    (B) is informative without bias
    (C) advocates musicals portraying social issues
    (D) is against musicals portraying social issues
    (E) is inflammatory

11. The people who wrote the words and music for the musicals

    (A) did not intend to explore racial prejudice
    (B) deliberately explored racial prejudice
    (C) had strong feelings against racial prejudice
    (D) were unconcerned about racial prejudice
    (E) There is not enough information to make a judgment.

12. Two-year colleges received a larger share of their total financial support from state funds and a smaller share from local governments in 1983–84 than they did in the previous year.

    From this we can conclude that

    (A) state governments will increase their influence on two-year colleges
    (B) state governments will decrease their influence on two-year colleges
    (C) local governments will increase their influence on two-year colleges
    (D) two-year colleges will have increased funding
    (E) two-year colleges will have decreased funding

13. Scotland is a kingdom united with England and Wales in Great Britain.

    We can conclude that

    (A) England is the same as Great Britain
    (B) Wales and England make up Great Britain
    (C) Scotland is part of England
    (D) Scotland is part of Great Britain
    (E) Scotland is not part of Great Britain

Questions 14 and 15

Quicksand pits are found in virtually every part of the world, but falling into one is seldom as horrible as it is depicted in stories.

14. Quicksand is found

    (A) practically everywhere
    (B) here and there
    (C) seldom
    (D) only in stories
    (E) in horrible parts of the world

15. The stories mentioned

    (A) have pictures of quicksand
    (B) have illustrations of quicksand
    (C) describe quicksand experiences

    (D) explain what quicksand is
    (E) give a realistic account of experiences with quicksand

16. One way to hold down the cost of auto insurance is to raise the amount of deductible costs you are willing to pay before the insurance company assumes financial responsibility. This can lower monthly premiums without risking the basic purpose of auto insurance—to cover losses you can't afford to absorb.

    Besides lower premium payments, what effect does a higher deductible have?

    (A) You pay less if there is damage.
    (B) You must pay more if there is damage.
    (C) You will have more total insurance.
    (D) Your insured amount will be more.
    (E) Your insured amount will be less.

Questions 17 to 21

COMPARISON OF AUTO INSURANCE COSTS

	With Usual Deductible	With Higher Deductible
Deductible	$150	$500
Monthly premium	$125	$100
Total coverage	$5,000	$5,000

17. How much will be saved in premiums over one year by taking a higher deductible?

    (A) $1,200
    (B) $300
    (C) $150
    (D) $125
    (E) $500

18. Sam chooses the higher deductible and has an accident with total damages of $1,000 after one year. You conclude that

    (A) he saves money with the higher deductible
    (B) he should have kept the usual deductible
    (C) the results would be the same with both policies
    (D) the policies cannot be compared
    (E) Sam should change insurance companies

19. What is Sam's total cost for insurance and repair of the accident in question 18 compared with what he would have paid on the usual deductible?

    (A) $350 more
    (B) $50 less
    (C) $350 less
    (D) $400 more
    (E) $50 more

20. If Sam (who has the higher deductible policy) has an accident that causes $7,000 damage to his car, he will have to pay

    (A) $7,000
    (B) $5,000
    (C) $2,500
    (D) $2,000
    (E) $500

21. Who will benefit the most from the policy he or she has chosen as opposed to the other policy?

	Person	Deductible	Repair costs per accident	Accidents per year
(A)	John	usual	$400	4
(B)	Harry	usual	$500	1
(C)	Sam	higher	$400	2
(D)	Betsy	higher	$4,000	1
(E)	Barbara	higher	$650	4

22. "Counting their toes and candles on birthday cakes are some of the ways that children can learn math." How can you use this information in the classroom?

    (A) Tell children that math can be used in everyday situations.
    (B) Teach more math in class.
    (C) Start teaching math at a higher level because children already know math.
    (D) Show how math can be used in everyday situations.
    (E) None of the above.

Questions 23 and 24

"Growth in state funds for colleges is expected to slow further in 1984."

23. This statement means that state funds for colleges

    (A) will increase in 1984
    (B) will decrease in 1984
    (C) will increase in 1984, but at a lower rate
    (D) will decrease in 1984, but at a lower rate
    (E) decreased during 1983

24. What action would you expect a college to consider because of the statement above?

    I.   decreasing enrollment
    II. seeking other sources of funding
    III. decreasing services to students

    (A) I
    (B) II
    (C) III
    (D) I and III
    (E) I, II and II

25. "There have been significant increases in four other types of health insurance provided by insurance companies." A logical conclusion is that

    (A) some types of health insurance have decreased
    (B) the previous sentence discussed a type or types of health insurance
    (C) all types of health insurance have increased
    (D) only four types of health insurance have increased
    (E) only insurance companies provide health insurance

26. The program was designed to ameliorate the financial condition of some of the students.

    Ameliorate means

    (A) lessen
    (B) eliminate
    (C) increase
    (D) make better
    (E) make worse

27. Driven by a high wind, dunes creep across deserts, forming a relentless tide of sand.

    Sand in the desert

    (A) can be controlled by planting shrubbery
    (B) stays in the same place
    (C) looks like waves
    (D) goes back and forth like a tide
    (E) cannot be controlled

28. "The Star-Spangled Banner" was written by F.S. Key in 1814. President Wilson ordered it played at military services in 1916. It was designated the national anthem by Act of Congress in 1931.

    (A) "The Star-Spangled Banner" was played at President Wilson's inauguration.

(B) "The Star-Spangled Banner" became the national anthem under President Wilson.
(C) President Wilson thought "The Star-Spangled Banner" should be our national anthem.
(D) "The Star-Spangled Banner" was written more than 100 years before being designated the national anthem.
(E) F.S. Key and President Wilson were acquaintances.

29. The coming of the railroads proved a boon to California agriculture.

We can conclude that

(A) the railroads were a problem for California farmers
(B) the railroads brought more people to California
(C) without the railroads, California agriculture would not have increased as rapidly as it did
(D) the railroads made products cheaper
(E) the railroads made products more expensive

30. "Not a ship escaped heavy damage," means:

(A) No ship had damage.
(B) Every ship had heavy damage.
(C) All ships had some damage, but not all had heavy damage.
(D) Some ships had heavy damage.
(E) Some ships had damage.

31. "Students learn more when they are praised." If you applied this statement in the classroom, you would

(A) praise each student for everything she does
(B) praise each student when he has done a good job
(C) praise at least one student every day
(D) praise each student at least once a week
(E) make the praise valuable by praising only in exceptional circumstances

Questions 32 and 33

When a cold air layer lies below a warm layer, mirage images appear above the real object. When the layers are reversed, the image is inverted below the real object.

32. Which drawing illustrates the above information?

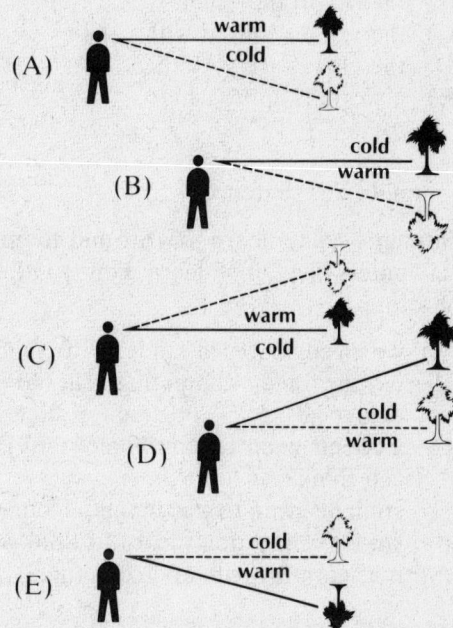

33. A mirage is

(A) an inversion
(B) an air layer
(C) a reversion
(D) an image
(E) an object

34. "People can have clean air if they demand it. The remedies for most forms of air pollution are known; they need only be applied."

This statement would be most stengthened by which of the following statements?

(A) The death rate has decreased in some cities.
(B) Pollution-control regulations have been passed.
(C) Smog-control devices are required in some states.

(D) Environmental lessons have been added to the curriculum in many schools.
(E) In several cities air-pollution-control programs are in effect with striking improvement of the air quality.

35. A canopy of clouds is spread across the sky. This means that

(A) the sky is clear
(B) the clouds are moving from one side of the sky to the other
(C) the sky is covered with clouds
(D) the clouds are very thick
(E) a storm is approaching

36. Complete this sentence:

"Students cannot learn to write and compute well unless they first learn how to think, therefore

(A) we need to teach students to think."
(B) writing and computing should be delayed."
(C) students need to stay home until they can think."
(D) students need to stay in school longer."
(E) students who don't learn to think cannot learn to write and compute."

37. Americans are said to consume too many "empty calorie foods." What does "empty calorie foods" refer to?

(A) foods that have no calories
(B) light foods
(C) foods that burn up their calories in the process of digestion
(D) junk food
(E) foods that have many calories but few vitamins, minerals or proteins

38. The greatest number of casualties in 1918 was not from the war but from a worldwide influenza epidemic that killed an estimated 20 million people throughout the world.

You can conclude that

(A) *casualties* and *deaths* are antonyms

(B) there were 20 million deaths in 1918
(C) there were fewer than 20 million deaths in 1918
(D) there were more than 20 million casualties during World War I
(E) there were more than 20 million deaths in 1918

39. What probable effect will a decreasing birthrate have on education?

I. Fewer teachers will be needed.
II. Fewer schools will be needed.
III. Fewer students will enroll.

(A) I
(B) II
(C) III
(D) II and III
(E) I, II and III

40. "Moderation in all things, including moderation" leads one to think that

(A) one should always be moderate
(B) one should sometimes be immoderate
(C) it is mediocre to be moderate
(D) moderation is dull
(E) moderation is modern

41. Earthquakes cause damage and loss of life, but scientists point out that they are vital to the continued development of our earth. Mountains are constantly eroding, and if they were not raised again, the world would become a place of stagnant seas and swamps.

The likely effect of the above information on a reader is

(A) no change in attitude
(B) that he will understand the benefits of earthquakes
(C) that he will be better prepared for earthquakes
(D) that he will understand that earthquakes are beneficial as well as harmful
(E) that he will know what to do in case of an earthquake

Questions 42 to 46

Years of Life Expected at Birth

Year	Total	Male	Female
1970	70.5	67.0	74.3
1960	69.7	66.6	73.1
1950	68.2	65.6	71.1
1940	62.9	60.8	65.2
1930	59.7	58.1	61.6
1920	54.1	53.6	54.6
1910	50.0	48.4	51.8
1900	47.3	46.3	48.3

42. The largest increase in total life expectancy is between

    (A) 1900 and 1910
    (B) 1910 and 1920
    (C) 1920 and 1930
    (D) 1930 and 1940
    (E) 1940 and 1950

43. What is the last census year in which a person who is still living in 1985 could have been born and outlived his or her expected life span?

    (A) 1900
    (B) 1910
    (C) 1920
    (D) 1930
    (E) 1940

44. A man born in 1950 can expect to live to the year

    (A) 2015
    (B) 2000
    (C) 2018
    (D) 2021
    (E) 2026

45. Which of the following are true, according to the chart?
    I. Women live longer than men.
    II. Life expectancy has increased every reporting period.
    III. Women have increased their life expectancy more than men.

    (A) I
    (B) I and II

(C) I and III
(D) I, II and III
(E) II

46. Projecting the information into the future, the following conclusion can be made:
    I. Life expectancy will increase, but at a slower rate.
    II. There will be an increasing number of older people.
    III. The life expectancy of men will decrease.

    (A) I
    (B) II
    (C) III
    (D) I and II
    (E) I, II and III

Questions 47 and 48

Red is the color of blood and excitement. Men who wear conservative, dark suits can be seen driving red sports cars, thereby revealing their inner selves. Red cars are more apt to be driven fast. Does the red car incite the person to drive fast or does the person who tends to drive fast choose a red car?

47. On the basis of the paragraph above, what conclusion can you draw?

    (A) Only people in red cars drive fast.
    (B) Only people in conservative suits buy red cars.
    (C) Only people in conservative suits drive fast.
    (D) People who drive fast choose red cars.
    (E) A person driving a red car is more apt to get a speeding ticket than someone driving a green car.

48. Which red items are symbolic of excitement?
    I. red roses
    II. bullfighters' capes
    III. fire engines
    IV. fire crackers

    (A) I and II
    (B) II, III and IV
    (C) II and III
    (D) III and IV
    (E) I, III and IV

49. Nuclear plants use large amounts of water for cooling. One likely effect of this is

    (A) a shortage of water
    (B) contamination of water
    (C) higher water temperatures downstream
    (D) fewer nuclear plants near water
    (E) higher humidity

50. More women are waiting to a later age to have children. The only certain conclusion that can be drawn from this is that

    (A) these women will have fewer children
    (B) these women will be more affluent
    (C) these mothers are more apt to be employed
    (D) there will be a temporary drop in school population
    (E) there will be more absenteeism on the job

MATHEMATICS
65 Minutes–50 Questions

Directions: Choose the best answer for each question and blacken the corresponding space on the Answer Sheet for Sample Test 1. The correct answers and explanations follow the test.

1. 1234.5678

   The 7 in the above number represents

   (A) ones
   (B) tens
   (C) tenths
   (D) hundredths
   (E) thousandths

2. Round off 76,569 to the nearest thousand.

   (A) 76
   (B) 77
   (C) 76,000
   (D) 76,500
   (E) 77,000

3. $\frac{7}{9}$ lies between each of the following pairs of numbers except

   (A) $\frac{2}{3}$ and $\frac{7}{2}$
   (B) $\frac{7}{11}$ and $\frac{9}{7}$
   (C) $\frac{1}{2}$ and 1
   (D) 0.7 and 0.9
   (E) $\frac{7}{8}$ and $\frac{8}{9}$

4. To check whether $\frac{x^2 - 4}{x + 2} = x - 2$, you could

   (A) multiply x − 2 by $x^2 - 4$
   (B) multiply x − 2 by x + 2
   (C) multiply x − 2 by x
   (D) multiply x + 2 by x
   (E) multiply x − 2 by 2

5. $16,752 \div 3 =$

   (A) has a remainder of 1
   (B) has a remainder of 2
   (C) has no remainder
   (D) cannot be divided
   (E) is smaller than 5,500

6. $\frac{1}{4} + \frac{1}{3} =$

   (A) $\frac{2}{7}$
   (B) $\frac{1}{12}$
   (C) $1\frac{2}{7}$
   (D) $\frac{7}{12}$
   (E) $1\frac{5}{12}$

7. $\frac{1}{12} - \frac{1}{16} + \frac{1}{20} =$

   (A) $\frac{17}{240}$
   (B) $\frac{3}{48}$
   (C) $\frac{1}{16}$
   (D) $\frac{1}{48}$
   (E) $\frac{3}{40}$

8. Which fraction is smallest?

   (A) $\frac{2}{3}$
   (B) $\frac{4}{9}$
   (C) $\frac{1}{2}$
   (D) $\frac{5}{11}$
   (E) $\frac{3}{7}$

9. $\frac{45}{54}$ reduced to its lowest terms is

   (A) $\frac{5}{9}$
   (B) $1\frac{1}{5}$
   (C) $\frac{2}{3}$
   (D) $\frac{1}{5}$
   (E) $\frac{5}{6}$

10. Change $\frac{1}{5}$ to a decimal.

    (A) 4.5
    (B) 5.4
    (C) 0.08
    (D) 0.80
    (E) 0.45

11. Which pair of numbers has a ratio of 4 to 11?

    (A) 49, 110
    (B) 16, 33
    (C) 77, 28
    (D) 28, 77
    (E) 110, 49

63

12. On an assignment, Sidney did 18 problems correctly and 6 incorrectly. The ratio of problems attempted to problems solved incorrectly is

   (A) 1:4
   (B) 4:3
   (C) 4:1
   (D) 3:4
   (E) 18:6

13. The scale on a house plan is 1:36. This means that

   (A) 1 in. = 36 yds
   (B) 1 ft = 6 yds
   (C) 1 ft = 3 yds
   (D) 1 in. = 1 yd
   (E) 1 in. = 3 yds

14. To get a B (80%) on a test, Susan had to answer at least 104 questions correctly. The number of questions on the test was

   (A) 140
   (B) 130
   (C) 107
   (D) 100
   (E) 64

15. What percent is 16 of 20?

   (A) 80%
   (B) $^{16}/_{20}$
   (C) 75%
   (D) 32%
   (E) 125%

16.

   A man 6 feet tall casts a shadow 5 feet long. The flagpole nearby casts a 15-foot shadow. How tall is the flagpole?

   (A) 11 ft
   (B) 15 ft
   (C) 18 ft
   (D) 21 ft
   (E) 26 ft

17. 28% of what number is 70?

   (A) 19.6
   (B) 142
   (C) 2.5
   (D) 98
   (E) 250

18. The prime factors of 60 are

   (A) 1, 2, 3, 5
   (B) 2, 3, 5
   (C) 1, 3, 4, 5
   (D) 12, 5
   (E) 6, 10

19. $\sqrt{4725}$ is closest to

   (A) 65
   (B) 68
   (C) 69
   (D) 75
   (E) 225

20. The temperature in Kevin's room has been fluctuating between 65° and 80°. The average temperature for the past five days has been 72°. What is the lowest average temperature the room can have for the week?

   (A) 65°
   (B) 70°
   (C) 72°
   (D) 75°
   (E) 80°

21. A person would be weighed in

   (A) milligrams
   (B) grams
   (C) kilograms
   (D) liters
   (E) meters

22. Convert 35° Celsius to Fahrenheit.

   (A) 7°
   (B) 20°
   (C) 52°
   (D) 67°
   (E) 95°

23. The basic rate for a telephone is $6 per month. Each call is charged at 30¢. How much will Nancy pay for March if she made 25 calls?

    (A) $6. 55
    (B) $13.50
    (C) $15.30
    (D) $15.75
    (E) $18.25

24. Sidney is baking 50 muffins. How many muffin tins will he need if there are 8 muffin cups in each tin?

    (A) 6
    (B) 6.25
    (C) 7
    (D) 8
    (E) 9

25. Tammy is the owner of a lamp store. A $50 lamp has been marked down 10% but hasn't sold. She decides to mark it down another 20%. What price will she put on it?

    (A) $20
    (B) $30
    (C) $35
    (D) $36
    (E) $40

26. Gudelia is five years older than Francis. Five years ago she was twice as old as Francis. How old is Francis?

    (A) 5
    (B) 10
    (C) 15
    (D) 20
    (E) none of these

27. The difference between a two-digit number and the number reversed is 36. The sum of the digits is 10. What is the number?

    (A) 56
    (B) 64
    (C) 73
    (D) 82
    (E) 91

28. Margaret borrowed $2,700 from the credit union to be paid back at the end of three years at 12% annual simple interest. How much will she pay back?

    (A) $972.
    (B) $2,700
    (C) $3,105
    (D) $3,672
    (E) $3,780

29. David filled a container that was 12 inches long by 8 inches wide, to a depth of 6 inches. How should he determine the number of cubic inches of water in the container?

    (A) $2(12 + 8 + 6)$
    (B) $8(6 + 12)$
    (C) $6(8 + 12)$
    (D) $12(6 + 8)$
    (E) $6 \times 8 \times 12$

30. Diane is going to put fringe around a tablecloth that is 3 feet by 5 feet. How many yards of fringe will she need to buy?

    (A) 16 yds
    (B) 2⅔ yds
    (C) 5 yds
    (D) 5⅓ yds
    (E) 10 yds

31. $(b - 4)(b + 3) =$

    (A) $b^2 - 12$
    (B) $2b - 1$
    (C) $b^2 - 1$
    (D) $b^2 - b - 12$
    (E) $b^2 - b + 12$

32. $8a - 4 = 60; a =$

    (A) 7
    (B) 7.5
    (C) 8
    (D) 15
    (E) 30

33. $3k^2 - 4k + 7 - 2k^2 =$

    (A) $k^2 - 4k + 7$
    (B) $-4k + 7$
    (C) $6k^2 - 4k + 7$
    (D) $-6k^4 - 4k + 7$
    (E) $-3k^5 + 7$

34. $3a^2 \times 4a^3 =$

    (A) $7a^5$
    (B) $12a^5$
    (C) $7a^6$
    (D) $144a^6$
    (E) $72a$

35. $678 + K - M - 401 = 385; K = 5M$. What is M?

    (A) 27
    (B) 108
    (C) 277
    (D) 18
    (E) 411

36. $x° + y° =$

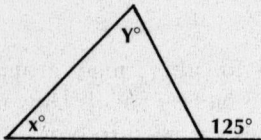

    (A) 55°
    (B) 62.5°
    (C) 90°
    (D) 125°
    (E) 180°

37.

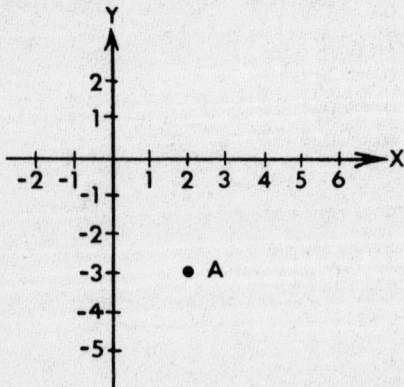

The coordinates of point A are

    (A) $X = 3, Y = 2$
    (B) $X = -3, Y = 2$
    (C) $X = 2, Y = -3$
    (D) $X = -2, Y = -3$
    (E) none of the above

38.

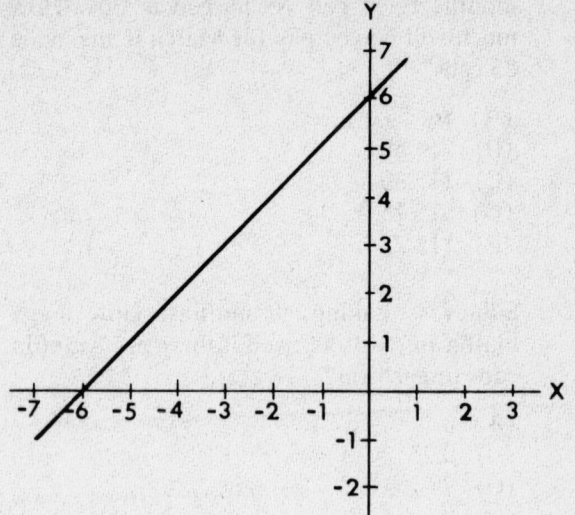

The equation for the above line is

    (A) $X - Y = 6$
    (B) $X + Y = 6$
    (C) $X = 6$
    (D) $Y = 6$
    (E) $Y - X = 6$

Questions 39 and 40

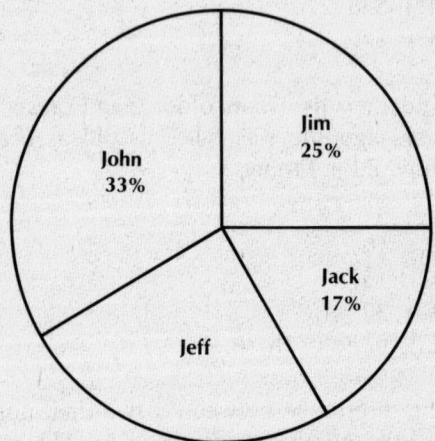

39. John, Jim, Jack and Jeff formed the Jay-Four company. Their investments in the company are shown in the pie graph above. What fraction of the total investment was Jeff's?

    (A) ⅓
    (B) ¼
    (C) ⅕
    (D) ⅙
    (E) 2/7

40. How many degrees does Jim's investment represent?

    (A) 25°
    (B) 50°
    (C) 75°
    (D) 90°
    (E) 100°

41. $\dfrac{4a - b}{2} =$

    (A) $2a - \dfrac{b}{2}$

    (B) $4a - \dfrac{1}{2}b$

    (C) $4a - \dfrac{b}{2}$

    (D) $2a - b$

    (E) $4a - b \div 2$

42. The formula for the area of a circle is $A = \pi r^2$. Find the area of a circle with a radius of 4.

    (A) 8
    (B) 4π
    (C) 16π
    (D) 8π
    (E) 16

43. Jason paid $11.60 for a shirt that was marked down by 20%. How much money did he save by buying at the sale price rather than the original price?

    (A) $2.00
    (B) $2.90
    (C) $2.32
    (D) $14.50
    (E) $11.60

44. If Kim throws three dice at one time, what are the chances that she will roll all sixes?

    (A) 3 in 6
    (B) 6 in 3
    (C) 1 in 18
    (D) 1 in 36
    (E) 1 in 216

45.

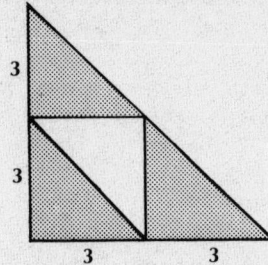

The formula for the shaded area is

    (A) $(3 \times 3 \times 3)^4$
    (B) $(3 \times 3 \times 3)^4 - (3 \times 3 \times 3)$
    (C) $\frac{1}{2} (3 \times 3 \times 3) \frac{3}{4}$
    (D) $\frac{3}{4} \times 3 \times 3$
    (E) $\frac{3}{4} \times \frac{1}{2} \times 6 \times 6$

46. James is arranging a display of coffee tins on a table 40 inches wide and 42 inches long. How many tins, each 6 inches in diameter, can be put on the surface of the table?

    (A) 42
    (B) 46
    (C) 47
    (D) 182
    (E) 186

47. There were 180 parents and students at graduation. At least a third of them were students. How many students attended?

    (A) 60–179
    (B) 60–180
    (C) 61–180
    (D) 120–179
    (E) 121–180

Questions 48 to 50

The community swim pool was being filled at a steady rate. The depth of the water was measured every 15 minutes and recorded in inches and centimeters.

Time	Inches	Centimeters
9:00 a.m.	7	17.92
9:15 a.m.	14	35.84
9:30 a.m.	21	53.76
9:45 a.m.	28	71.86
10:00 a.m.	35	89.60
10:15 a.m.	42	107.52

48. At which time was an incorrect measurement logged?

    (A) 9:15
    (B) 9:30
    (C) 9:45
    (D) 10:00
    (E) at no time

49. At the same rate, when will the water in the pool be 7 feet deep?

    (A) 10:30

    (B) 11:00
    (C) 11:15
    (D) 11:45
    (E) 12:00

50. How deep will the water be at noon?

    (A) 6 ft
    (B) 7 ft
    (C) 7 ft 7 in.
    (D) 8 ft
    (E) more than 8 ft

WRITING
60 Minutes–Two Essays

Directions: You have 30 minutes for each of two essays. The essay topics are intended to measure how well you write, given limitations on time and subject. Quality is more important than quantity. Spend some of your time organizing your thoughts. Supporting statements and examples should be specific. Write only on the assigned topic. Write legibly and within the lines provided. Space for notes is provided below.

Topic A
John Molloy found that students reacted differently when he dressed casually from the way they reacted when he dressed more formally. From your observations and experiences, relate how what you wear affects you and others and how you would use this information.

Topic B
Do you agree or disagree with the statement, "Good teachers are born, not made"? Support your position with examples from your experience with teachers you have met.

TOPIC A

_____

_____

_____

_____

_____

_____

_____

_____

_____

_____

_____

_____

_____

_____

_____

_____

_____

_____

_____

_____

_____

_____

TOPIC B

_____

_____

_____

_____

_____

_____

_____

_____

_____

_____

_____

_____

_____

_____

_____

_____

_____

_____

_____

_____

_____

_____

ANSWERS TO SAMPLE TEST 1

READING

1. D	11. B	21. A	31. B	41. D
2. A	12. A	22. D	32. B	42. C
3. D	13. D	23. C	33. D	43. C
4. C	14. A	24. E	34. E	44. A
5. A	15. C	25. B	35. C	45. D
6. B	16. B	26. D	36. A	46. D
7. C	17. B	27. E	37. E	47. E
8. E	18. B	28. D	38. E	48. B
9. E	19. E	29. C	39. E	49. C
10. B	20. C	30. B	40. B	50. D

MATHEMATICS

1. E	11. D	21. C	31. D	41. A
2. E	12. C	22. E	32. C	42. C
3. E	13. D	23. B	33. A	43. B
4. B	14. B	24. C	34. B	44. E
5. C	15. A	25. D	35. A	45. E
6. D	16. C	26. B	36. D	46. A
7. A	17. E	27. C	37. C	47. A
8. E	18. B	28. D	38. E	48. C
9. E	19. C	29. E	39. B	49. D
10. D	20. B	30. D	40. D	50. C

SCORING OF SAMPLE TEST 1

Each institution or state decides on the passing score. In general, 35 correct on the reading and 33 correct on the mathematics sections will be passing.

How to score the writing The writing section is scored holistically, which makes it difficult to grade. You may want to have someone else score it and make suggestions on how to improve your writing, or you may want or need to score it yourself.

Here is a suggestion: start with a total of 50 points for each essay. You will then subtract as follows for errors.

Subtract

- 1½ points for every line that you wrote over the limit
- 1 point for every punctuation, spelling or minor grammatical error
- 3 points for each major grammatical error, incorrectly used word or paragraph error
- 5 points for low vocabulary level or jargon
- 10 points if your arguments don't support your statement
- 10 points if you did not have a conclusion
- 25 points if you didn't stay on the topic

This will give you a raw score for each essay. Add the two raw scores together to get your total. You need a total score of 75 points to pass.

EXPLANATION OF ANSWERS TO SAMPLE TEST 1

READING

1. **D** The insecticide had good and bad effects and they were far-reaching.

2. **A** Insecticides kill insects. The target insects in this case were mosquitoes; cockroaches were killed accidentally. Mosquitoes spread malaria.

3. **D** None of the other answers is certain.

4. **C** *Belief* fits best.

5. **A** *Wise* may come to mind, but it is not a definition of *civil*.

6. **B** Rivers of wind have widespread effects on weather.

7. **C** $1,200 + 1,985 = 3,185$

8. **E** Remember your history or add $2,800 + -1,200$ (B.C.) $= 1,600$ (A.D.).

9. **E** A crevasse is a deep cut in ice or rock.

10. **B** No advocacy or bias is shown.

11. **B** "The messages were slipped in," but we don't know what opinions they expressed.

12. **A** Who pays, says. No other statement is logical.

13. **D** England, Scotland and Wales make up Great Britain.

14. **A** *Virtually* means *practically*.

15. **C** *Depict* means *describe*.

16. **B** A higher deductible means that you pay more for repairs before the insurance company starts paying.

17. **B** $25.00 per month or $25 \times 12 = 300 per year.

18. **B** He saves $300 in premiums, but pays $500 − $150 = $350 more deductible, for a loss of $50.

19. **E** See 18, above.

20. **C** He pays the first $500. He is insured for $5,000, so he will have to pay any amount over that: $7,000 − $5,000 = $2,000. Altogether he will have to pay $2,500.

21. **A** Best bets are the usual policy and several accidents, or higher deductible and few accidents. Eliminate B, C and E. This is a time-consuming problem, so if you're short of time, choose A or D and move on.

Check A:

Usual

Premiums	$125 × 12 =	$1,500
Deductible	$150 × 4 =	600
Total Cost		$2,100

Higher

Premiums	$100 × 12 =	$1,200
Deductible	$400 × 4 =	1,600
Total Cost		$2,800

$700 saving

Check D:

Usual

Premiums	$125 × 12 =	$1,500
Deductible	$150 × 1 =	150
Total cost		$1,650

Higher

Premiums	$100 × 12 =	$1,200
Deductible	$500 × 1 =	500
Total Cost		$1,700

$50 saving

22. **D** "Show" beats "tell."

23. **C** Growth has decreased, but it's still growth.

24. **E** They will "consider" all three, but perhaps act only on II.

25. **B** "Other" is the key word.

26. **D**

27. **E** *Relentless* means steady and persistent; unremitting. The implication is that the movement of the sand cannot be stopped.

28. **D** $1931 - 1814 = 117$

29. **C** A "Boon" is a benefit.

30. **B** If no ships escaped heavy damage, then every ship had heavy damage.

31. **B** Students sense when praise is not deserved.

32. **B** Both drawings below are correct.

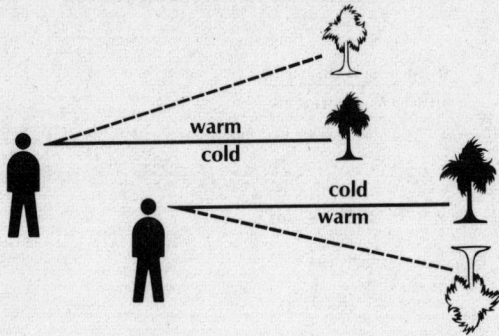

33. **D** The passage refers to "mirage images."

34. **E** Only E illustrates the argument.

35. **C** A canopy is a cover.

36. **A** This answer should be obvious to you.

37. **E** The foods have calories but must lack something; E fits best.

38. **E** The 20 million flu deaths plus the number of war casualties in 1918.

39. **E** If there are fewer children, there will be fewer students, and fewer teachers and schools will be needed.

40. **B** Even moderation has to be tempered, which means that sometimes one should not be moderate.

41. **D** Choice A is possible, but D is more likely.

42. **C** Look for a large difference.

   (A) about 3   (D) about 3
   (B) about 4   (E) about 5
   (C) about 5

   Work out C and E.

43. **C** Underline *last*. Add the year and life expectancy. It has to be less than 1985.

44. **A** $1950 + 65.6 = 2015.6$

45. **D** All are true.

46. **D** I and II are valid. III is doubtful.

47. **E** "Red cars are more apt to be driven fast."

48. **B** Red roses are lovely but are not particularly symbolic of excitement.

49. **C** Choice C is the most logical. Using the water for cooling means the water will be heated; fish live in waters having a narrow temperature range.

50. **D** This is the only certainty.

MATHEMATICS

1. **E** See page 29.

2. **E** 76,569
   5 or more, round up.
   1,000
   77,000

3. **E** Compare by cross-multiplication.

   (A) $\dfrac{2}{3} \times \dfrac{7}{9} \times \dfrac{3}{2}$ 18 21 14 27

   (B) $\dfrac{7}{11} \times \dfrac{7}{9} \times \dfrac{9}{7}$ 63 77 49 81

   (C) $\dfrac{1}{2} \times \dfrac{7}{9} \times \dfrac{1}{1}$ 9 14 7 9

   (D) $\dfrac{7}{10} \times \dfrac{7}{9} \times \dfrac{9}{10}$ 63 70 70 81

   (E) $\dfrac{7}{8} \times \dfrac{7}{9} \times \dfrac{8}{9}$ 63 56 63 72 $\dfrac{7}{9}$ is smaller than both

4. **B** To check $\frac{12}{3} = 4$, you would multiply 3 by 4. Similarly, you would multiply $(x + 2)$ by $(x - 2)$ to check.

5. **C** $1 + 6 + 7 + 5 + 2 = 21$, which is divisible by 3; therefore, 16,752 is divisible by 3 and has no remainder.

6. **D** $\frac{1 \times 3}{4 \times 3} + \frac{1 \times 4}{3 \times 4} = \frac{3 + 4}{12} = \frac{7}{12}$

7. **A** $\frac{1}{12} - \frac{1}{16} + \frac{1}{20} = \frac{20}{240} - \frac{15}{240} + \frac{12}{240} = \frac{17}{240}$

8. **E** Compare by cross-multiplication.

   $\frac{2}{3}$ 18 ⤬ 12 $\frac{4}{9}$ $\frac{4}{9}$ is smaller

   $\frac{4}{9}$ 8 ⤬ 9 $\frac{1}{2}$ $\frac{4}{9}$ is smaller

   $\frac{4}{9}$ 44 ⤬ 45 $\frac{5}{11}$ $\frac{4}{9}$ is smaller

   $\frac{4}{9}$ 28 ⤬ 27 $\frac{3}{7}$ $\frac{3}{7}$ is smallest

   With this type of question, first check to determine whether there are any answers you can eliminate, e.g., ⅔ is 0.67, ½ is 0.50.

9. **E** $^{45}/_{54} \div \frac{2}{3} = {}^{15}/_{18} \div {}^{2}/_{3} = {}^{5}/_{6}$

10. **D** $5\overline{)4.00}$ .80

11. **D** First look for the smaller number to be placed first. Eliminate C and E. Next, is the first number divisible by 4? Eliminate A. Is the second number divisible by 11? Try B: $^{16}/_4 = 4$; $^{33}/_{11} = 3$; no. Try D: $^{28}/_4 = 7$; $^{77}/_{11} = 7$; yes.

12. **C** Problems attempted : incorrect problems
    $$18 + 6 : 6$$
    $$24 : 6$$
    $$4 : 1$$

13. **D** Convert to same measure.
    (A) 1 in. = 36 × 36 in.
    (B) 1 ft = 6 × 3 ft
    (C) 1 ft = 3 × 3 ft
    (D) 1 in. = 36 in.
    (E) 1 in. = 3 × 36 in.

14. **B** $\frac{80\%}{100\%} = \frac{104}{n}$ $n = \frac{104(100)}{80}$
    $$80n = 104(100) \quad n = 130$$

15. **A** $\frac{\text{is}}{\text{of}} = \frac{16}{20} \times 100 = 80\%$

16. **C**

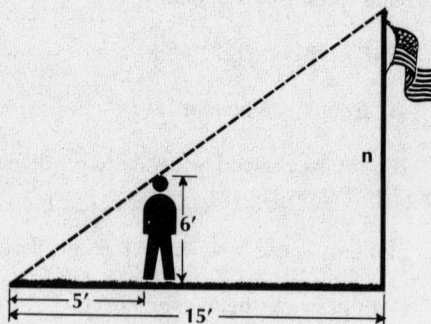

$\frac{\text{man}}{\text{shadow}} = \frac{\text{flagpole}}{\text{shadow}}$

$$\frac{6}{5} = \frac{n}{15}$$
$$6 \times 15 = 5n$$
$$\frac{6 \times 15}{5} = n$$
$$18 = n$$

17. **E** $\frac{\text{is}}{\text{of}} = \frac{70}{28} \times 100 = 250$

18. **B**
2	60	A. 1 is not prime.
2	30	C. 1 and 4 are not prime.
3	15	D. 12 is not prime.
5	5	E. 6 and 10 are not prime.
	1	

19. **C** $\sqrt{\overline{47}\,\overline{25}}$

    1. 2 places in answer; eliminate E.
    2. square root closest to 47 is 6 ($6^2 = 36$); eliminate D.
    3. 47 is close to 49, so try 68 or 69.

20. **B** The lowest temperature will be less than 72; eliminate C, D, E.
    $$5 \times 72 = 360$$
    $$2 \times 65 = \underline{130}$$
    $$490$$
    $$\frac{490}{7} = 70$$

21. **C** Pounds are equivalent to kilograms.

22. **E** C ➡ F larger; eliminate A, B.

Approximation	**Formula**
$2C + 30° = F$	$9/5\,C + 32° = F$
$2 \times 35° + 30° = 100°$	$9/5(35)° + 32° = 95°$

23. **B** $6.00 + 25 \times 0.30 = 6.00 + 7.50 = 13.50$

24. **C** $50 \div 8 = 6¼$ He'll need 7.

25. **D** 10% off = 90% $\$50 \times 0.9 = \$45$
    20% off = 80% $\$45 \times 0.8 = \$36$

26. **B** A. Five years ago Francis was less than a year old; eliminate.
    B. Substitute 10 for Francis.

    Now: $G = 15, F = 10$
    5 years ago: $15 - 5 = 2(10 - 5)$
    $10 = 2 \times 5$ yes

27. **C** Is the sum of the digits 10? Eliminate A. Subtract the digits reversed. Look for 36.

    B   64   C   73
       -46 -37
       $\overline{18}$ $\overline{36}$

28. **D** Total to be repaid is more than amount borrowed; eliminate A and B.
    Total   = Principal + Interest
    Interest = Principal × Rate × Time

    $= \$2,700 \times \dfrac{12}{100} \times 3 = \$972$

    Total = $\$2,700 + \$972 = \$3,672$

29. **E** Volume $= l \times w \times h$
    $= 12 \times 8 \times 6$

30. **D** Perimeter $= 2(l + w)$
    $= 2(3 + 5)$
    $= 2(8) = 16$ ft
    16 ft ÷ 3 = 5⅓ yds

31. **D** $= b^2 - b - 12$
    $-b$

32. **C** $8a - 4 = 60$
    Add 4: $+ 4 = +4$
    Divide by 8: $\overline{8a\quad = 64}$
    $a = 8$

33. **A** $3k^2 - 4k + 7 - 2k^2 =$
    $3k^2 - 2k^2 - 4k + 7 =$
    $k^2 - 4k + 7$

34. **B** $3a^2 \times 4a^3 = (3 \times 4)\, a^{(2+3)} = 12a^5$

35. **A** Estimate: $700 + 4M - 400 = 400$
    $300 + 4M = 400$
    $4M = 100$
    $M = 25$

    Eliminate B, C and E.
    Now solve the problem
    $678 + K - M - 401 = 385;\ K = 5M$
    Substitute $678 + 5M - M - 401 = 385$
    Combine $678 - 401 + 4M = 385$
    $277 + 4M = 385$
    Subtract 277 $\underline{-277 \qquad -277}$
    $4M = 108$
    Divide by 4 $M = 27$

36. **D** The exterior angle equals the sum of the two opposite interior (inside) angles. The three inside angles of a triangle add up to 180°.

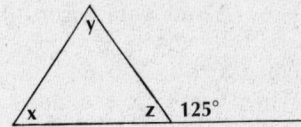

    $x + y + z = 180°$
    $z + 125° = 180°$
    $x + y + z = z + 125°$
    $\underline{-z \qquad -z}$
    $x + y = 125°$

37. **C**

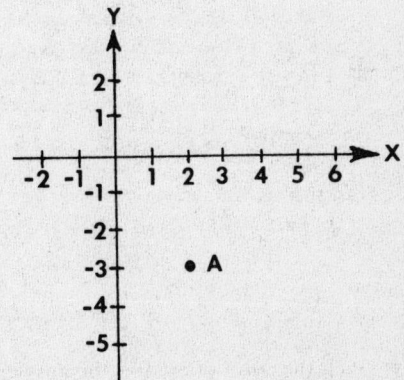

    The X direction is listed first, then Y.
    A is 2 units to the right (+) along X, hence X = 2
    A is 3 units down (−) along Y, hence Y = −3

38. **E**

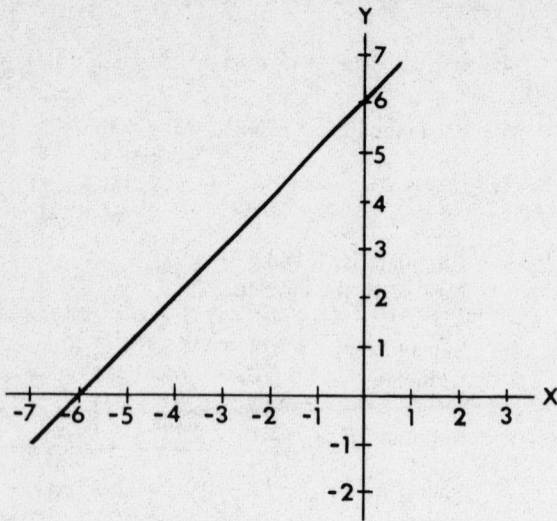

When X is 0, Y is 6
When Y is 0, X is −6
Try out the choices.
(A) Cover X with your finger (0)
$$-Y = 6 \text{ or } Y = -6$$
Cover Y with your finger (0)
$$X = 6; \quad \text{no}$$
(B) When $X = 0 \quad Y = 6$
When $Y = 0 \quad X = 6$; no
(C) vertical
(D) horizontal
(E) When $Y = 0, -X = 6$ or $X = -6$
When $X = 0, Y = 6$; yes

39. **B**

$$
\begin{array}{ll}
33\% & \\
17\% & 100\% \\
+25\% & -75\% \\
\hline
75\% \text{ others} & 25\% \text{ Jeff} = \frac{1}{4}
\end{array}
$$

40. **D** $\dfrac{25\%}{100\%} = \dfrac{d°}{360°}$

$\dfrac{25 \times 360}{100} = d° = 90°$
Or 25% is ¼
$\frac{1}{4} \times 360° = 90°$

41. **A** $\dfrac{4a - b}{2} = \dfrac{4a}{2} - \dfrac{b}{2} = 2a - \dfrac{b}{2}$ or $2a - \frac{1}{2}b$.

Pick the form offered in the answer choices.

42. **C** $A = \pi r^2$
$= \pi 4^2$
$= 16\pi$

43. **B** $\dfrac{\text{part}}{\text{whole}} = \dfrac{\$11.60}{p} = \dfrac{80\%}{100\%}$ (marked down 20%)

$\dfrac{\$11.60 \times 100}{80} = p = \$14.50$

Saving is $\$14.50 - \$11.60 = \$2.90$
or $\$14.50 \times 20\% = \$2.90$

Another method: Saving is $\dfrac{20\%}{80\%} = \dfrac{p}{\$11.60}$ or ¼
of $11.60

$\dfrac{20 \times \$11.60}{80} = p = \$2.90$

44. **E** 1 die − 1 chance in 6
2 dice − 1 chance in 6 on each = $6 \times 6 = 36$
3 dice − 1 chance in 6 on each = $6 \times 6 \times 6 = 216$

45. **E** There are two ways of doing this.

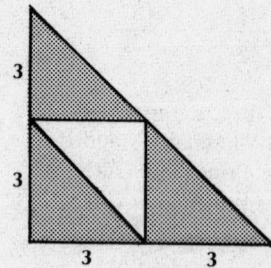

Method 1. Use this when there are three shaded triangles equal in area.

$A = \frac{1}{2}$ bh

One Δ: $A = \frac{1}{2} \times 3 \times 3 = \dfrac{9}{2}$

Three Δ: $A = 3 \times \dfrac{9}{2} = \dfrac{27}{2}$

Which choice is the same? E.

Method 2. The shaded area is $\dfrac{3}{4}$ of the large triangle.

$A = \frac{1}{2}$ bh
$= \frac{1}{2} \times 6 \times 6$

Shaded area $= \dfrac{3}{4} \times \dfrac{1}{2} \times 6 \times 6$

46. **A**

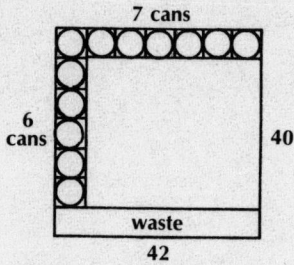

$42 \div 6 = 7$ tins in a row
$40 \div 6 = 6\frac{2}{3}$ rows
Number of cans $= 6 \times 7 = 42$
(You can't put $\frac{2}{3}$ of a tin on the table.)

47. **A** $180 \div 3 = 60$
There were at least 60 students. There was at least one parent. The number of students was 60 to 179.

48. **C** Look for a discrepancy. There is none in time or inches, but there is one in centimeters. The error occurred at 9:45.

Time	Change	In	Change	Centi- meters	Change
9:00		7		17.92	
	15		7		17.92
9:15		14		35.84	
	15		7		17.92
9:30		21		53.76	
	15		7		18.10
9:45		28		71.86	
	15		7		17.74
10:00		35		89.60	
	15		7		17.92
10:15		42		107.52	

49. **D** It fills at 28 inches per hour.
$$\frac{7 \text{ ft} \times 12}{28} = 3 \text{ hrs to fill to 7 ft}$$

The pool started being filled at   8:45
Add   3:00 hr
—————
11:45

50. **C** Refer to question 49.
At 11:45 the depth will be 7 ft.
At 12:00 the depth will be 7 ft 7 in.

SAMPLE TEST 2

Sample Test 2 is similar to the Arizona test. You can also use this test to practice for tests given in Alabama, Colorado, Georgia, Indiana, Kentucky, Missouri, Nebraska and South Carolina. The professional-knowledge section can be used to study for any state test that has a professional-knowledge component.

You have 130 minutes for the basic skills test, which includes reading, grammar and mathematics. Distribute your time as you think best. Don't spend more than 40 minutes on any section until you have completed the other sections. Tackle your best subject first. If you have no preference, do the mathematics and grammar first, as they take less time. Then answer the reading questions.

In some of these state tests the test-makers have followed the practice of repeating an entire reading-comprehension passage word for word before asking another set of questions about the passage. I have varied the passages in this sample test, but you should be aware that you may run into such identical reading selections.

You have 90 minutes for the professional-knowledge test. On this test, as in the reading, grammar and mathematics tests, the number of answer choices offered may vary from question to question.

You need 120 correct answers on the grammar, reading and math section and about 48 correct answers on the professional-knowledge section in order to pass.

infer: to conclude by reasoning from something known or assumed,
to imply

imply = to have as a necessary part, condition etc
to indicate indirectly
hint, suggest.

Directions: Choose the best answer for each question and blacken the corresponding space on the Answer Sheet for Sample Test 2. The correct answers and the explanations follow the test.

READING (50 Questions)

1. Many animals, such as canines, felines and ursines, are carnivorous.
   Carnivorous means

   (A) doglike
   (B) catlike
   (C) meat-eating
   (D) plant-eating
   (E) eating everything

2. What she calls experience is but fatigue and cynicism.
   In the above sentence *but* means

   (A) if not
   (B) yet
   (C) except
   (D) positively
   (E) merely

3. The person who believes in the saying, "I had rather wear out than rust out" would most likely

   (A) take frequent short vacations rather than one long vacation
   (B) retire early and have several hobbies
   (C) live in an arid climate
   (D) not retire
   (E) supplement her diet with iron

4. Brown University students have no required courses outside their majors. The effect of this policy on students is that

   (A) they can take whichever courses they like
   (B) they don't have to be concerned about which courses they take
   (C) they have less choice of courses
   (D) they have more responsibility for selecting courses
   (E) they have no guidance in selection of courses

5. Our society, recently based on mass production, education, communication, consumption and political movements, is now becoming "demassified."
   In this sentence *demassified* means

   (A) smaller
   (B) individualized
   (C) polarized
   (D) antireligious
   (E) split

Questions 6 and 7

Delaware began as a confederacy of three counties. Descending in size and ascending in population, they are Sussex, Kent and New Castle.

6. New Castle is the county that is

   (A) largest and most populous
   (B) largest and least populous
   (C) smallest and least populous
   (D) smallest and most populous
   (E) middle-sized and most populous

7. Kent is

   (A) bigger than Sussex and more populous than New Castle
   (B) smaller than Sussex and more populous than New Castle
   (C) bigger and less populous than New Castle
   (D) smaller and less populous than New Castle
   (E) smaller and less populous than Sussex

8. "The problem with the coastal bay," said the captain with salty exaggeration, "is that you can get out and walk almost anywhere." This means that

   (A) the bay is too salty
   (B) the water in the bay is so salty that you can walk on it
   (C) the bay is too salty to swim in
   (D) the surface of the water in the bay is smooth as glass
   (E) the bay is exceedingly shallow

9   Although two thirds of all living creatures can fly, man was earthbound until this century.
Choose the most correct statement:

(A) Birds constitute two thirds of all creatures.
(B) Man was descending until this century.
(C) Man did not fly until this century.
(D) In this century a third of men have learned to fly.
(E) Only 30% of all creatures cannot fly.

10. In the race for survival, the star tortoise bears the handicap of beauty.
This means that

(A) the star tortoise is slow but beautiful
(B) its beauty reduces the star tortoise's chances for survival
(C) star tortoises are raced
.(D) star tortoises will become extinct
(E) racing star tortoises are handicapped according to their beauty

11. The mountains in California usually receive more than 25 inches of precipitation a year, the majority of it as snow.
In other words,

(A) more than 25 inches of snow fall annually
(B) 25 inches of snow fall anually
(C) 12½ inches of snow fall annually
(D) more than half the precipitation is rain
(E) more than half the precipitation is snow

Questions 12 and 13

It rose in the southwest, and in about two minutes, before reaching the opposite horizon, it had broken up into about twenty pieces.

12. *It* refers to

(A) a dust storm
(B) a meteorite
(C) a satellite
(D) an airplane
(E) There is not enough information to answer.

13. Where is "the opposite horizon"?

(A) northeast
(B) northwest
(C) southeast
(D) southwest
(E) not enough information given

14. Nine tenths of icebergs are below the surface. Like icebergs, walruses are seen by people who are looking mostly above the surface.
We can infer that

(A) walruses are mostly on the surface
(B) icebergs and walruses are mostly on the surface
(C) there is much we don't know about icebergs and walruses
(D) walruses are never seen underwater
(E) icebergs can't be seen underwater

15. The river Thames bisects the city of London.
Most precisely, this means that

(A) the Thames divides London into halves
(B) the Thames divides London into parts
(C) the Thames divides London into two parts
(D) the Thames cuts through London
(E) the Thames bypasses the city of London

16. The caddisfly larva is making an evolutionary leap, from a waterbound to a landcrawling insect, in search of a better food supply. The larvae leave the streams at night to feed on waterfront plants. Of 10,000 species of caddisfly, only three have larvae that live on land. These species may be going through a change like one the ancestors of other insects went through thousands of years ago.
It is reasonable to assume that

(A) caddisfly larvae leap
(B) other caddisfly species will soon be land-dwellers
(C) the larvae stay on land during the day
(D) the larvae never return to the water
(E) evolution thousands of years ago resulted partly from a need for new food sources

17. Average college costs, including tuition, will increase by ten percent this year. Most colleges have designated part of the tuition-increase revenues for student financial aid. This means that

    (A) the tuition increase will go to help some students
    (B) all students will pay ten percent more for college this year
    (C) part of the tuition increase some students pay will go to pay other students' tuition and expenses
    (D) tuition at all colleges will increase ten percent
    (E) *designated* is synonymous with *designed*

18. The island of Bora Bora looms from the sea like a cathedral, its triumvirate of brooding peaks sweeping down to white beaches and a lagoon whose colors shimmer from midnight blue to topaz.
    From this we gather that

    (A) the lagoon is extremely blue
    (B) the island has three mountain peaks
    (C) the island peaks are falling into the lagoon
    (D) the island is low in comparison to its size
    (E) there is no vegetation on Bora Bora

Questions 19 and 20

Migrating birds have a wide variety of sensory abilities. Daytime migrants use their vision to steer by the sun, aided by a precise sense of time. Night fliers take compass cues from star patterns. Homing pigeons see ultraviolet and polarized light and can hear low-frequency sounds that emanate from distant surf. It is believed that migrating birds tune in on the earth's magnetic field in combination with gravity to establish their direction. Birds are excellent weather sensors, waiting for the passage of fronts that bring favorable winds. How a bird determines its position remains a mystery to man, however.

19. We conclude that

    (A) a great deal of study has been done about migratory bird life
    (B) we know nothing about migrating birds' abilities to determine their location

    (C) homing pigeons use the earth's magnetic field to get direction
    (D) all migrating birds steer by the sun
    (E) we have complete knowledge of how a bird determines its position

20. Birds use all of the following to determine location except

    (A) star patterns
    (B) the earth's magnetic field
    (C) weather fronts
    (D) gravity
    (E) the sun

21. A study has shown that of every two hundred people who go on a diet, only ten will achieve their weight loss goal, and of those ten, only one will stay at that weight.
    We can conclude that

    (A) diets are successful
    (B) most people don't have willpower
    (C) diets are generally unsuccessful
    (D) only 5% of dieters will stay at their goal weight
    (E) only 0.5% of dieters will reach their goal weight

22. Alice Liddell, daughter of an Oxford University dean and friend of the author-artist, inspired the character depicted in Lewis Carroll's *Alice's Adventures in Wonderland*. *Alice's Adventures in Wonderland* was illustrated by

    (A) an Oxford dean
    (B) a friend of the author-artist
    (C) Alice Liddell
    (D) Alice Lewis
    (E) Lewis Carroll

23. "Lisa could but smile at his discomfiture," is most close in meaning to

    (A) Lisa smiled at his discomfiture.
    (B) Lisa could not smile at his discomfiture.
    (C) Lisa could only smile at his discomfiture.
    (D) Lisa couldn't help smiling at his discomfiture.
    (E) Lisa did something other than smile at his discomfiture.

24. Who could have imagined the numerous benefits to consumers from space exploration—dishes and cooktops that do not expand, contract or crack under extreme temperature variations, made of the same material as nose cones of spacecraft; and telephone conversations relayed by satellites.
We can infer that

   (A) scientific exploration often yields unexpected benefits
   (B) space exploration is a waste of time
   (C) space exploration is a waste of money
   (D) dishes and cooktops benefit spacecrafts
   (E) the benefits of space exploration are imaginary

Questions 25 and 26

As a result of the energy crisis, we have worked diligently to make our homes more energy-efficient. We have weatherstripped, insulated and sealed them to the best of our abilities. We may have done too good a job. These very measures contribute to pollution indoors. Some homes have air-pollution rates so high that they would be illegal outdoors. Air-conditioning systems and humidifiers spread lung ailments, especially where windows are sealed. Burning colored paper in a fireplace gives off arsenic vapor. Cooking in a gas stove will cause a pollution level equal to that of Los Angeles on a smoggy day.

25. We can conclude that

   (A) in trying to solve one problem, we may have introduced another
   (B) weatherstripping is not energy-efficient
   (C) the majority of stoves in Los Angeles use gas
   (D) fireplaces give off arsenic poisoning
   (E) people have not been concerned with energy efficiency

26. The quickest remedy for indoor pollution is

   (A) installing air conditioning
   (B) installing a humidifier
   (C) weatherstripping
   (D) installing more insulation
   (E) good ventilation

27. The number of 18-year-olds peaked last year and will have declined by 33% by 1995; however, the proportion of 18-year-olds entering higher education is expected to rise by 15%. Therefore, institutions of higher education can anticipate that by 1995 there will be

   (A) more students
   (B) fewer students
   (C) the same number of students
   (D) other changes which will negate the projections
   (E) none of the above

28. Bread is such an essential part of life that it has entered the language in many ways, such as *breadwinner, breaking bread, nation's breadbasket, knows which side his bread is buttered on,* and *bread* meaning money. Which expression means *cognizant of the source of one's income*?

   (A) breadwinner
   (B) breaking bread
   (C) bread
   (D) knows which side his bread is buttered on
   (E) nation's breadbasket

29. Age is the stock-in-trade, the nemesis and the glory of models.
As far as models are concerned, age is

   (A) only beneficial
   (B) two sides of a coin
   (C) only detrimental
   (D) traded like stocks
   (E) glorious

30. The number of lawyers has doubled every ten years for the past thirty years in the United States. If this trend continues, it will result in a decrease in the average number of cases handled by each lawyer.

   (A) Sentences 1 and 2 are both fact.
   (B) Sentences 1 and 2 are both opinion.
   (C) Sentence 1 is fact and sentence 2 is opinion.
   (D) Sentence 1 is opinion and sentence 2 is fact.

31. In the next ten years, the American labor force is likely to become increasingly dominated by semiskilled service jobs. We should expect the number of white-collar jobs to grow faster than total employment. The number of blue-collar jobs will grow more slowly.

    (A) Sentences 1, 2 and 3 are fact.
    (B) Sentences 1, 2 and 3 are opinion.
    (C) Sentences 1 and 2 are fact; sentence 3 is opinion.
    (D) Sentences 1 and 3 are fact; sentence 2 is opinion.

32. There are nearly two hundred people killed each year by lightning. Many of them could have survived if they had taken cover during thunderstorms. During a storm, it is dangerous to be on a golf course; in a boat; swimming; atop a hill; at the beach; under an isolated tree; near a wire fence, clothesline, overhead wire or towers; or riding a bike, tractor, horse or farm machinery. If you are outdoors during a thunderstorm, you are safe in a car, in a grove of trees or in a ditch.

    (A) Sentences 1, 2, 3, and 4 are fact.
    (B) Sentences 1, 2, 3 and 4 are opinion.
    (C) Sentence 1 is fact; sentences 2, 3 and 4 are opinion.
    (D) Sentences 1 and 2 are fact; sentences 3 and 4 are opinion.

Questions 33 to 35

The following sentences are not in order. Decide in what order they should be, and answer questions 33–35.

1. Large particles have been spotted around Vega, a star 150 trillion miles away in the constellation Lyra.
2. Astronomers hope to use it to look at novae, pulsars, neutron stars, black holes and galaxies similar to the Milky Way.
3. Because it could see light from 14 billion years ago—which has been speeding toward Earth ever since—it might even witness traces of the "Big Bang" that some astronomers think created the universe.
4. The "stellar debris" may be turning into planets and moons—the first actual evidence of a possible solar system of record-making size.

5. One astronomer thinks the most exciting finds will be those things we just don't think of at all.
6. It may unlock the secret of quasars, those powerful beacons that appear to be at the edge of the cosmos.
7. Discovery of what may be a new planetary system offers only a hint of the dramatic findings in store as astronomers peer farther and farther into the universe.
8. In the future, scientists hope to gain unlimited vision of the cosmos by placing a space telescope beyond Earth's atmosphere.
9. The telescope will focus on objects seven times farther away than can be seen by the best ground-based instruments.

33. The first sentence of the passage should be sentence number

    (A) 1   (C) 5
    (B) 3   (D) 7

34. The middle sentence of the passage should be sentence number

    (A) 3   (C) 7
    (B) 5   (D) 9

35. The last sentence of the passage should be sentence number

    (A) 1   (C) 5
    (B) 3   (D) 7

Questions 36 to 40

Which is the correct alphabetical order for the words below?

36. 1. mildness   3. misfortune
    2. middle   4. militarily

    (A) 1,2,3,4
    (B) 4,3,2,1
    (C) 2,1,4,3
    (D) 3,2,1,4

37. 1. foliage   3. folly
    2. folk   4. fondly

    (A) 1,2,3,4
    (B) 2,3,1,4
    (C) 1,3,4,2
    (D) 3,2,1,4

38. 1. optional   3. organization

     2. orally   4. orange

     (A) 2,1,3,4
     (B) 1,2,4,3
     (C) 1,3,4,2
     (D) 4,3,1,2

39. 1. attack   3. attribution

     2. attraction   4. attain

     (A) 1,2,4,3
     (B) 2,1,4,3
     (C) 4,1,2,3
     (D) 1,4,2,3

40. 1. trust   3. trunk

     2. tumult   4. tune

     (A) 1,2,3,4
     (B) 2,4,3,1
     (C) 3,1,2,4
     (D) 4,2,1,3

Questions 41 to 45

In the following questions you will be given guide words on a dictionary page. Pick out the word that would not be on the page.

41. guide words: magnificent–mailer

    (A) majestic
    (B) magnify
    (C) mail
    (D) magnolia

42. guide words: cloud–clung

    (A) club
    (B) cloy
    (C) clown
    (D) clunk

43. guide words: riprap–riviera

    (A) rivulet
    (B) riproaring
    (C) riverhouse
    (D) rival

44. guide words: status–steam

    (A) staves
    (B) stealth
    (C) stature
    (D) steak

45. guide words: lose–louver

    (A) loss
    (B) lout
    (C) lots
    (D) loose

Questions 46 to 50

The following questions give you a part of a word. Choose the part that correctly completes the word.

46. -ancipated

    (A) am
    (B) em
    (C) im
    (D) emm

47. -gardless

    (A) re
    (B) ire
    (C) irre
    (D) ere

48. sli-

    (A) page
    (B) ppage
    (C) ppige
    (D) pege

49. ski-

    (A) lful
    (B) lfull
    (C) llful
    (D) llfull

50. irresist-

    (A) able
    (B) eble
    (C) ible
    (D) ibel

MATHEMATICS (50 Questions)

1. 2.09 + 202.99 + 2209.9 + 20209.02 =

   (A) 20,635.09
   (B) 22,624
   (C) 22,624.09
   (D) 20,634.19

2.
$$\begin{array}{r} 123 \\ 1,467 \\ 4,301 \\ 106,709 \\ 217,683 \\ + \quad 73 \\ \hline \end{array}$$

   (A) 330,356
   (B) 310,366
   (C) 303,356
   (D) 33,356

3. The temperature in Kay's room fluctuated between 71 degrees and 74 degrees during the week. What could the average temperature *not* be?

   (A) 72
   (B) 73
   (C) 74
   (D) 75

4. 1 inch = 2.54 cm. How many inches are there in 7 cm?

   (A) 17.78
   (B) 2.76
   (C) 7.62
   (D) 1.78

5. If baby food is on sale for 7 cans for $1.26, how much would a case of 56 jars cost?

   (A) $8.82
   (B) $70.56
   (C) $.18
   (D) $10.08

6. There are 100 centimeters in 1 meter. How many square centimeters are there in 3 square meters?

   (A) 30,000
   (B) 900,000
   (C) 300
   (D) 900

7.
$$\begin{array}{r} 59.8 \\ \times 0.97 \\ \hline \end{array}$$

   (A) 579.96
   (B) 57.996
   (C) 58.006
   (D) 5800.6

8. $\frac{7}{8} \times \frac{1}{21} =$

   (A) $\frac{28}{167}$
   (B) $\frac{11}{29}$
   (C) $\frac{1}{6}$
   (D) $\frac{5}{6}$

9. $\frac{7}{8} + \frac{2}{3} =$

   (A) $\frac{9}{11}$
   (B) $1\frac{1}{2}$
   (C) $\frac{14}{24}$
   (D) $1\frac{13}{24}$

10. $\frac{5}{6} - \frac{1}{4} =$

   (A) $\frac{4}{2}$
   (B) $\frac{7}{12}$
   (C) $\frac{1}{3}$
   (D) $\frac{13}{12}$

11. Brand A beets cost $.69 a can, brand B cost $.73, brand C cost $.58 and Brand D cost $.64. What is the average cost of a can of beets?

   (A) $.66
   (B) $.67
   (C) $.58
   (D) $.73

12.

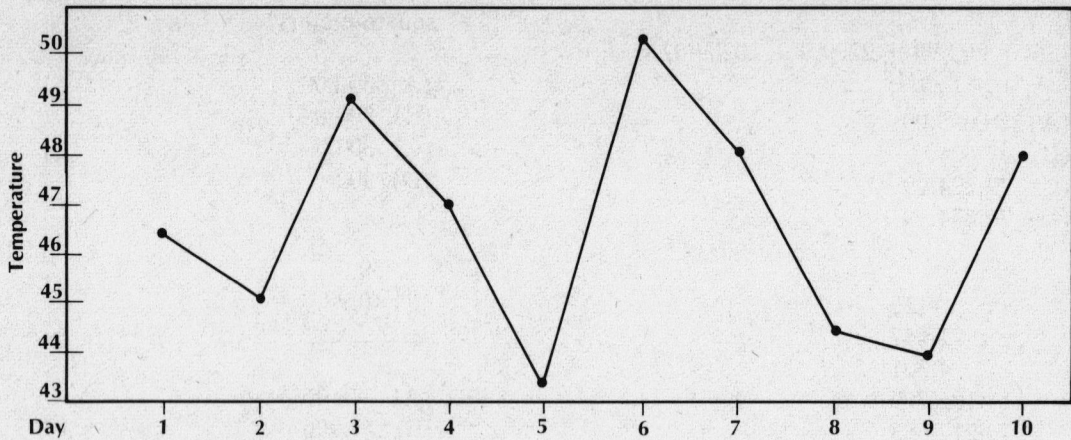

On how many days was the temperature lower than 45 degrees?

(A) 3
(B) 4
(C) 5
(D) 6

13. Bob drove from 9:36 a.m. until 4:27 p.m. How long did he drive?

(A) 6 hr, 51 min
(B) 7 hr, 51 min
(C) 7 hr, 4 min
(D) 5 hr, 4 min

14. Multiply 4 gallons 2 quarts 1 pint 6 ounces by 3.

(A) 12 gal 6 qt 3 pt 18 oz
(B) 14 gal 2 oz
(C) 12 gal 8 qt 1 pt 2 oz
(D) 12 gal 6 qt 4 pt 8 oz

15. If the perimeter of a square is 64, what is the length of each side?

(A) 8
(B) 16
(C) 32
(D) 48

16. 0.068 =

(A) 6.8%
(B) 68%
(C) 0.68%
(D) .068%

17.
$$\begin{array}{rllll} & 4 \text{ gal} & 2 \text{ qt} & 1 \text{ pt} & 6 \text{ oz} \\ - & 3 \text{ gal} & 2 \text{ qt} & 1 \text{ pt} & 7 \text{ oz} \end{array}$$

(A) 1 gal 3 qt 1 pt 7 oz
(B) 1 gal 3 qt 1 pt 1 oz
(C) 3 qt 1 pt 15 oz
(D) 3 qt 3 pt 9 oz

18. Diane is going to put fringe around a tablecloth that is 4 ft by 6 ft. How many feet of fringe will she need?

(A) 20 ft
(B) 24 ft
(C) 10 ft
(D) 14 ft

19. 16,752 ÷ 3

(A) has a remainder of 1
(B) has a remainder of 2
(C) has no remainder
(D) is smaller than 5,500

20. $\frac{2}{3} + \frac{3}{4} =$

(A) $\frac{5}{7}$
(B) $\frac{5}{12}$
(C) $\frac{12}{17}$
(D) $\frac{17}{12}$

21. $49/56$ reduced to lowest terms is

    (A) $1/4$
    (B) $1\,1/4$
    (C) $6/7$
    (D) $7/8$

22. $0.0847 \div 7 =$

    (A) 0.0121
    (B) 0.121
    (C) 1.210
    (D) 0.00121

23. Change $2/5$ to a decimal.

    (A) 2.5
    (B) 0.04
    (C) 0.40
    (D) 0.25

24. The basic rate for a telephone is $5.75 per month. Each call is charged at $.35. How much will John's October telephone bill be if he made 27 calls?

    (A) $5.75
    (B) $15.20
    (C) $9.45
    (D) $6.10

25. Change $1/8$ to percent.

    (A) 12%
    (B) 8%
    (C) 12.5%
    (D) 0.125%

26.

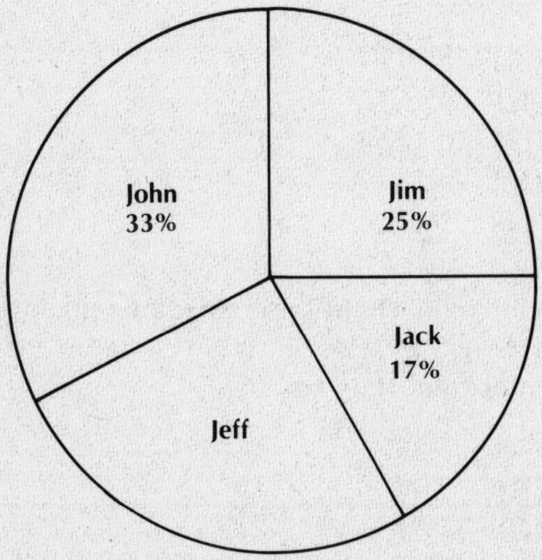

John, Jim, Jack and Jeff formed the Jay-Four Company. Their investments in the company are shown in the graph above. What fraction of the total have Jim and Jeff invested?

    (A) $1/3$
    (B) $1/2$
    (C) $1/5$
    (D) $1/4$

27. $100 \div 0.25 =$

    (A) 2,500
    (B) 4
    (C) 40
    (D) 400

28. Change 0.56 to a fraction.

    (A) 56
    (B) $5\ 6/10$
    (C) $28/100$
    (D) $14/25$

29. Change $9/20$ to a decimal.

    (A) 0.18
    (B) 1.80
    (C) 0.9
    (D) 0.45

30. $7/9$ equals

    (A) $9/63$
    (B) $42/54$
    (C) $7/21$
    (D) $87/114$

31. Packages are delivered every four days, Monday through Friday. If packages were delivered on Thursday, what is the next date for delivery?

    (A) Monday
    (B) Tuesday
    (C) Wednesday
    (D) Thursday

32. $2{,}862 \div 6$ is exactly

    (A) 473
    (B) 474
    (C) 476
    (D) 477

33. 1.85 changed to percent is

    (A) 1.85%
    (B) 18.5%
    (C) 185%
    (D) 0.0185%

34. 50,422 + 1,578 + 396 + 9,242 + 85 =

    (A) 283,222
    (B) 61,723
    (C) 149,230
    (D) 61,623

35. At the end of March Karen's electric meter showed 7,064 kilowatt hours. At the end of April it showed 7,295 kwh. How many kwh did she use during April?

    (A) 14,359
    (B) 231
    (C) −231
    (D) 269

36. During the first five months of the year the total rainfall was 47.08 inches. It rained 9.023 inches in June, 6.971 in July, 0.0076 in August and 2.105 in September. What was the total rainfall for the first nine months of the year?

    (A) 65.7673 in.
    (B) 22.883 in.
    (C) 65.1866 in.
    (D) 65.1146 in.

37. Vince Johnson paid $8,799 for his car three years ago. If it depreciates at the rate of $1,271.47 per year, what is the car worth now?

    (A) $4,984.59
    (B) $12,613.41
    (C) $3,814.41
    (D) $7,527.53

38. Jeanne bought a blouse on sale for 20% off. She paid $11.60, while the original price was $14.50. How much did she save by buying the blouse on sale?

    (A) $2.00
    (B) $26.10
    (C) $3.10
    (D) $2.90

39.   80,682
       −   49,893
       ‾‾‾‾‾‾‾‾‾‾‾

    (A) 30,789
    (B) 30,575
    (C) 31,789
    (D) 30,899

40. $6\frac{3}{10} - 3\frac{5}{16} =$

    (A) $3\frac{1}{10}$
    (B) $2\frac{59}{80}$
    (C) $2\frac{79}{80}$
    (D) $2\frac{21}{80}$

41. What is the product of 176 and 28?

    (A) 204
    (B) 148
    (C) 3,918
    (D) 4,928

42.   5,008
       ×   79
       ‾‾‾‾‾‾‾‾‾‾‾

    (A) 485,776
    (B) 395,632
    (C) 40,132
    (D) 3,950,632

43. The high-school baseball team had a winning average of 0.725. What percent of their games did they win?

    (A) 0.725%
    (B) 7.25%
    (C) 72.5%
    (D) 725%

Questions 44 and 45

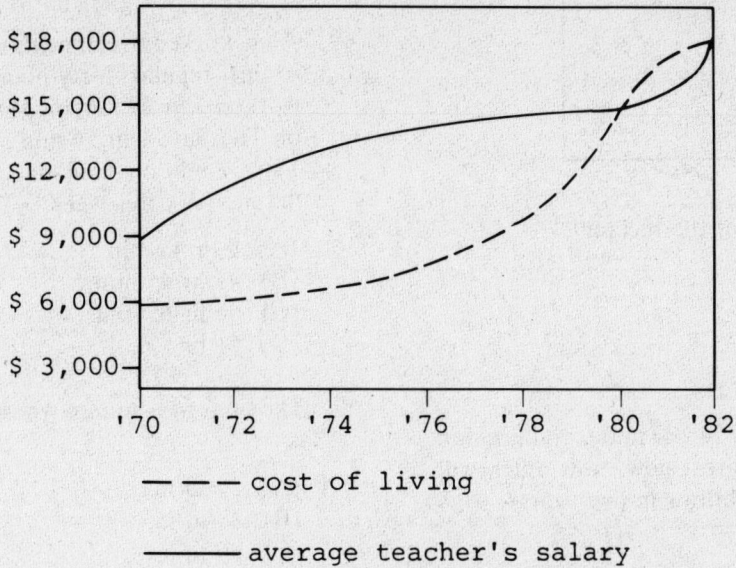

— — — cost of living

————— average teacher's salary

44. In which year was the average teacher's salary less than the cost of living?

(A) 1978
(B) 1980
(C) 1981
(D) 1982

45. How much was the average teacher's salary in 1980?

(A) $15,000
(B) $18,000
(C) $9,000
(D) $6,000

46.

Monthly Unemployment Rate

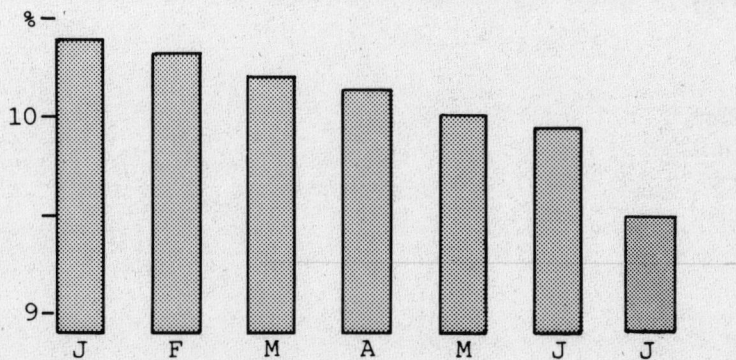

The unemployment rate in July was

(A) 10.5%
(B) 105
(C) 9.5%
(D) 9%

47.

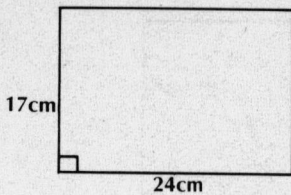

17cm

24cm

What is the area of the rectangle?

(A) 41 cm^2
(B) 48 cm^2
(C) 508 cm^2
(D) 408 cm^2

48. If Sharon deposits $4,000 in the credit union at 6% annual interest now, how much will she be able to withdraw in five years?

(A) $1,200
(B) $4,000
(C) $5,200
(D) $4,240

49. Alan worked overtime this week. In addition to his regular forty-hour work week, he worked 3 hr 29 min on Monday, 2 hr 43 min on Tuesday, 1 hr 56 min on Wednesday and 1 hr 37 min on Thursday. How many hours did he work this week?

(A) 9 hr 45 min
(B) 49 hr 45 min
(C) 50 hr 65 min
(D) 51 hr 5 min

50. The area of a square whose side is 29 inches is

(A) 29 sq in.
(B) 48 sq in.
(C) 96 sq in.
(D) 841 sq in.

GRAMMAR *(50 Questions)*

1.

Average cost in U.S. dollars					
	England	**Germany**	**Italy**	**Holland**	**France**
Hotel room	$67	$50	$52	$41	$60
Breakfast	$ 8	$ 3	$11	$ 7	$ 8
Dinner	$18	$20	$18	$22	$18

In which country can one eat most inexpensively?

(A) England   (B) Germany   (C) Holland   (D) France

2. Which is the correct spelling?

(A) reciept   (C) receept
(B) receipt   (D) receit

3. Which words in the following book title should be capitalized?

$$\underline{the\ rise\ and\ fall\ of\ rio}$$
$$1\quad 2\quad 3\quad\ 4\quad 5\quad 6$$

(A) 1, 3, 5   (C) 2, 4, 6
(B) 1, 2, 3, 4, 5, 6   (D) 1, 2, 4, 6

4. I can't decide between these two cars. Either _____ excellent.

(A) seem
(B) seems

5. Jerry _____ hardly stop laughing.

(A) couldn't
(B) could
(C) could not
(D) wouldn't

6.

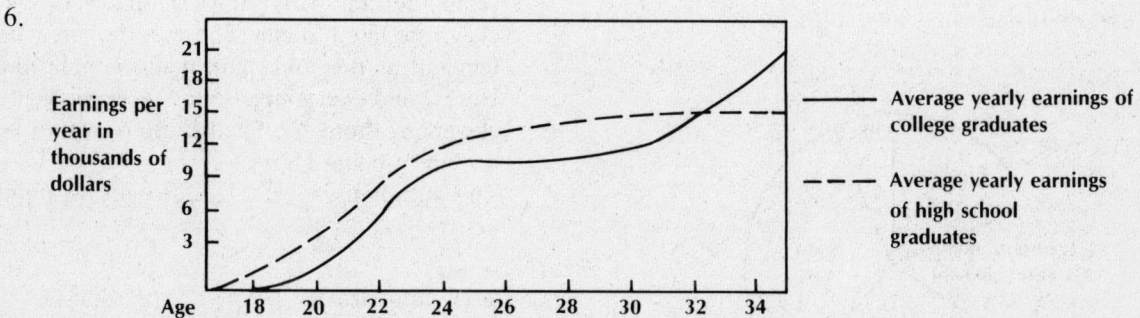

At what age do high school and college graduates earn the same amount?

(A) 20
(B) 24
(C) 28
(D) 32

7. Lucille was once given a monogrammed
   _____ .

   (A) hankerchief
   (B) handkercheif
   (C) hankercheif
   (D) handkerchief

8. Which words should be capitalized in the
   following sentence?
   on wednesday sally and i saw the birds flying
    1   2   3   4

   south for the winter.
    5   6

   (A) 1, 2, 3, 4, 6
   (B) 1, 2, 3, 4, 5, 6
   (C) 1, 2, 3, 4, 5
   (D) 1, 2, 3, 4

9. Neither Horace _____ Harry wanted
   the job, since it meant relocating.

   (A) or
   (B) nor
   (C) neither

10. _____ your birthday!

    (A) Its
    (B) It's
    (C) Its'

11. There was no way of knowing the _____
    the election would have.

    (A) affect
    (B) effect

12.

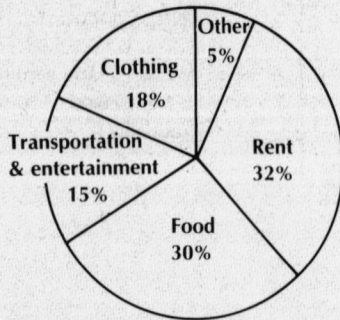

The diagram shows how Russ spends his
money. Russ spends the most on

(A) rent
(B) food
(C) clothing, transportation and entertain-
    ment
(D) clothing and other

13. Martha was able to complete the report with
    the help of her many _____ .

    (A) assistance
    (B) assistents
    (C) assistants

14. All juniors at Hanover High School take
    English, French, Chemistry I and Physics.
    Which word should not be capitalized?

    (A) Chemistry
    (B) French
    (C) Physics

15. Harry was the kind of fellow who was always
    fun to be around. He told the latest jokes
    and always had some witty comment when-
    ever he saw you. Sheila was not the same.
    She didn't tell jokes, and no one could
    remember any witty things she had said, but
    everyone liked Sheila. She was the one who
    laughed at the jokes and made people like
    Harry, and everyone else too, feel witty and
    clever. Without the Sheilas, there would be
    no fun in being Harry.
    The author uses _____ to get his point
    across.

    (A) comparison
    (B) detail
    (C) reason
    (D) explanation

16. Which drawing illustrates a mirage resulting
    from a warm air layer below a cold air layer
    in which the image appears inverted below
    the real object?

real object ———— [tree] image -------- [tree]

(A) [figure]

(B) [figure]

(C) [figure]

(D) [figure]

(E) [figure]

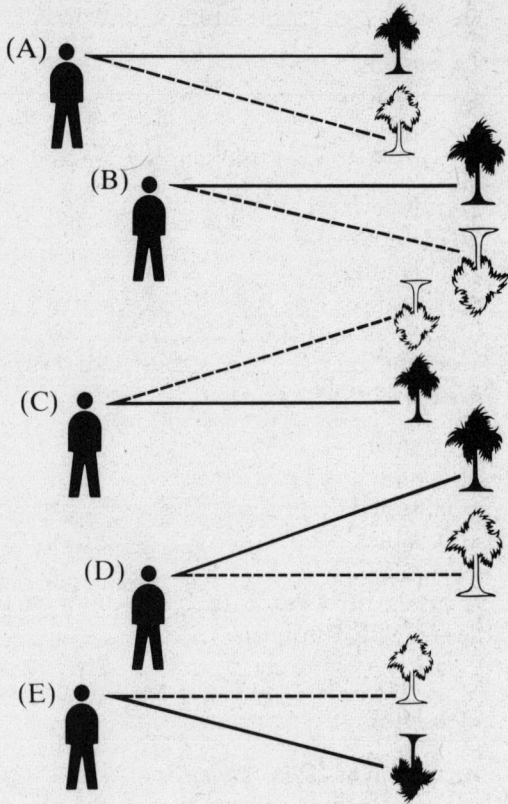

17. You could accuse him of being many things, but not of being _____ .

(A) vane
(B) vein
(C) vain

18. Lawrence told doctor jones that he wanted
                   1   2

    to become a doctor.
                 3

    Which word(s) should be capitalized?

    (A) 1, 2, 3
    (B) 1, 2
    (C) 2

19. Bernie acts as though he _____ already the vice-principal.

    (A) was
    (B) were

20. You should not use _____ equipment. It is too valuable.

    (A) there
    (B) their
    (C) they're

21. The northeastern part of the state is _____ .

    (A) mountanous
    (B) mountainous
    (C) mountanious
    (D) mountaneous

22. I didn't know to _____ he was speaking.

    (A) who
    (B) whom

23. One of _____ boys will be captain of the team.

    (A) this
    (B) these

24. He _____ his orange juice every morning.

    (A) drink
    (B) drank
    (C) drunk

25. The book was given to both _____ .

    (A) you and me
    (B) me and you
    (C) I and you
    (D) you and I

26. The antonym for *none* is

    (A) nothing
    (B) something
    (C) some
    (D) one

27. A synonym for *stationery* is

    (A) unmoving
    (B) terminal
    (C) writing paper

28. She had _____ her engagement to him.

    (A) break
    (B) breaked
    (C) broke
    (D) broken

29. Mr. Bradley likes you and _____ .

    (A) he
    (B) him

30. A synonym for *viscosity* is

    (A) thinness
    (B) thickness
    (C) viciousness
    (D) gutsiness

31. The opposite of *urban* is

    (A) suburban
    (B) city
    (C) rural
    (D) sophisticated

32. Where would you find recent articles on educational reform?

    (A) an encyclopedia
    (B) *The World Almanac*
    (C) *Reader's Guide to Periodical Literature*
    (D) an education textbook

33. She was the most _____ girl in town.

    (A) happy
    (B) happiest

34. Every boy wanted _____ own watch.

    (A) his
    (B) their

35. Fill in the blanks with the appropriate words. She could do nothing _____ _____ the award.

    (A) accept except
    (B) except except
    (C) accept accept
    (D) except accept

36. The sidewalks were already melting as the sun _____ like a fireball out of the east.

    (A) rise
    (B) rose
    (C) risen

37. He was _____ himself with worry.

    (A) beside
    (B) besides

38. A word that means the same as *trepidation* is

    (A) lukewarm
    (B) cautious
    (C) courage
    (D) fear

39. Who had _____ Mrs. Evertrue's necklace?

    (A) steal
    (B) stole
    (C) stoled
    (D) stolen

40. A group of boys _____ waiting at the door, ready for lunch.

    (A) was
    (B) were

41. An antonym of *horizontal* is

    (A) level
    (B) vertical
    (C) horizon
    (D) surface

42. The synonym for *recall* is

    (A) remember
    (B) revoke
    (C) forget
    (D) ignore

43. Ed is a meek lamb, now that he is under Susan's supervision. This is an example of a

    (A) simile
    (B) metaphor

44. The faculty at Rand Intermediate School is expected to advise activities and supervise events. Each activity and event is weighted according to the time involved as follows: coaching a sport or pep squad, supervising the yearbook, three points each; advising

student government, supervising convocations or rallies, two points each; all other advising or supervision, one point each. Each faculty member is expected to handle six points.
The above passage uses primarily

(A) comparison
(B) detail
(C) reason
(D) explanation

45. In which reference work would you look to find the annual amount of rainfall in Peru?

(A) *The Farmer's Almanac*
(B) a dictionary
(C) an encyclopedia
(D) an atlas

46. He ran like a deer.
This is an example of a

(A) simile
(B) metaphor

47. For the first time in more than a decade, enrollments in teacher-education programs are growing. Education is becoming more attractive, because students are realizing how important education is to our nation's future. More undergraduates are transfer-ring into colleges of education and fewer are transferring out. The increase in enrollment is encouraged by teacher shortages in some fields and in some parts of the country. The shortages present some interesting possibilities for new teachers.
The main topic of the above passage is

(A) teacher shortages
(B) increased enrollments
(C) the importance of education
(D) more students planning to teach

48. When Louis became angry, he was a raging volcano.
This is an example of

(A) simile
(B) metaphor

49. *Urbane* means the same as

(A) witty
(B) city
(C) sophisticated
(D) countrified

50. Her face was as white as a sheet.
This is an example of a

(A) simile
(B) metaphor

PROFESSIONAL KNOWLEDGE
90 Minutes–73 Questions

Directions: Choose the best answer for each question and blacken the corresponding space on the Answer Sheet for Sample Test 2. The correct answers and the explanations follow the test.

1. State colleges received a larger share of their total financial support from the federal government and a smaller share from the state governments last year than they did in the previous year.
   From this we can conclude that

   (A) the federal government will increase its influence on state colleges
   (B) the federal government will decrease its influence on state colleges
   (C) state governments will increase their influence on colleges
   (D) colleges will have decreased funding

2. Counting their toes and candles on birthday cakes are some of the ways that children can learn math.
   This is an example of

   (A) a frivolous, nonsensical use of math
   (B) applied theory
   (C) tactile theory
   (D) how math can be used in everyday situations

3. Private donations to colleges are expected to decrease in 1987. With this in mind, what action(s) would you expect colleges to consider?

   (A) decreasing enrollment
   (B) finding other sources of funding
   (C) decreasing services to students
   (D) all of the above

4. Praise should be used in the classroom

   (A) with restraint, to retain its value
   (B) whenever a student has done something well
   (C) lavishly, since none of us can get too much
   (D) on a daily basis; find something good to praise each day

5. The factor that has the strongest influence on how much a class will learn is

   (A) the teacher's enthusiasm
   (B) the teacher's knowledge
   (C) the students' interest in the subject
   (D) the students' willingness to learn

6. An effective way to encourage junior high school students to read more is for the teacher to

   (A) make classics available in the classroom
   (B) have a mandatory "reading hour" each day
   (C) require one book report each week
   (D) let the students read anything they want to in their spare time

7. More women are waiting to a later age to have children. The possible results of this that may affect schools are that

   (A) these women will have fewer children
   (B) these women will be more affluent
   (C) these mothers are more likely to be employed
   (D) all of the above

8. Teachers have been role models since teaching began. At times it has not been conscious. At times teachers and others have denied it. But whether it is emphasized or denied, the fact cannot be escaped. Since students spend at least six hours a day with a teacher, that teacher's personality will have an effect on students.
   Which statement is not supported by the philosophy of the above passage?

   (A) Teachers should have training in affective behavior.
   (B) Psychology is as essential to teachers as educational methods.
   (C) How teachers act toward each other affects students.
   (D) What teachers do on their own time has no effect on students.

Questions 9 to 11

Research has shown that class discipline is different when a teacher dresses more formally.

9. When a teacher is dressed more formally, one could expect class discipline to be

   (A) better
   (B) worse
   (C) unchanged
   (D) confused

10. You could expect the research conclusions to be in favor of

   (A) less formal dress in the classroom
   (B) more formal dress in the classroom
   (C) making no change in dress
   (D) uniforms for students

11. If she paid attention to these research findings, a teacher preparing to substitute-teach an unruly class would

   (A) dress as usual
   (B) dress to identify her unique personality
   (C) dress casually, to show empathy with the students
   (D) dress formally, to facilitate discipline

12. Most teachers correct with red pen or pencil. Red is often linked with blood or anger. Students have been heard to say, "My paper is bleeding." We hear, "I was so mad, I saw red." In light of this information, the most logical suggestion would be that

   (A) red be used for correcting when a teacher is angry
   (B) red be used when a student makes or repeats an irritating mistake
   (C) a color other than red be used for correcting
   (D) black ink be used for correcting

13. In a successful learning situation

   (A) the teacher knows what the objective is
   (B) the students know what the objective is
   (C) the teacher and the students know what the objective is
   (D) the teacher has told the students what the objective is

14. One school district's policy is, "The teacher's primary objective should be to act as a role model for students." A teacher working in this school district would expect that

   (A) his personal life would need to be circumspect
   (B) what he does outside school hours is his own business
   (C) he should be pals with the students
   (D) he would have to be married

15. The challenge facing education is how to respond to tradition without either rejecting it or becoming its slave.
This statement advocates

   (A) tradition
   (B) rejection
   (C) facing challenges
   (D) a middle course

16. An increasing number of students are transferring from four-year colleges to community-college job-training programs. We can conclude that

   (A) four-year colleges don't provide a good education
   (B) one needs four years of college to enroll in a job-training program
   (C) community colleges are better than four-year colleges
   (D) the transfer students are seeking specific job training

Questions 17 and 18

Children who are listened to are likely to be better behaved. Since children are not adept at conversation, a technique called active listening can help. Most people already use this technique but don't employ it with children. Active listening encourages the person to talk with responses such as, "And then what happened?" Another technique is to use a reflexive question. A child says, "I want to go home." You respond, "You want to go home?" The child replies, "Yes, I'm sleepy." This gives you the reason the child wants to go home.

17. A reflexive question

   (A) is an automatic response
   (B) reflects in question form what the speaker said

    (C) is a question about oneself
    (D) is a question upon which the speaker has had time to reflect

18. Which statement agrees with the above passage?

    (A) Children can't discern whether you are listening to them or not.
    (B) Uncommunicative teenagers probably have a background of one-way communication.
    (C) Children think most adults listen to them.
    (D) Dominating speech by a parent increases communication.

19. The U.S. Census Bureau reports that the average lifetime earnings for a woman with a bachelor's degree is $523,000. A male high-school graduate will earn $861,000. Female high-school graduates will earn $381,000, while a man with a bachelor's degree will get $1,190,000. The conclusion is that

    (A) a man without a college degree will earn less than a woman with a college degree
    (B) it is not financially beneficial for a woman to attend college
    (C) a woman with a bachelor's degree will earn less than a man without a college education.
    (D) a woman with a bachelor's degree will earn more than a man with a high-school degree

20. Some school districts are experimenting with a four-day school week, each school day being longer to equal the time of instruction during a five-day week. All of the following are possible advantages except:

    (A) savings on teachers' salaries
    (B) savings on transportation and utilities
    (C) more enthusiasm
    (D) less absenteeism due to conflicting doctor and dental appointments

Questions 21 and 22

Active listening reaps big rewards. People who have attended listening seminars are better workers. They interact with others more effectively and make fewer mistakes, thus saving time. Think of the important meetings you have attended that have been delayed by someone who arrived an hour late because he didn't ascertain the correct starting time. Much money is lost when a major project has to be redone because a staff member failed to listen to instructions. If each of the more than 100 million members of the U.S. work force made one $10 error each year because of poor listening, the cost would be more than $1 billion.

21. Active listening can result in all of the following benefits except:

    (A) fewer meetings
    (B) saving money
    (C) better workers
    (D) fewer mistakes

22. The above information could be applied by a teacher in each of the following ways except

    (A) including a unit on listening in an English class
    (B) actively listening to students
    (C) actively listening in meetings
    (D) explaining the theory of active listening to a third-grade class

Questions 23 to 26

A basic tenet of competency-based education is that the teacher must articulate the goal of the course. The goal is broken down into a number of concrete competency objectives. A test that clearly reflects the objectives is developed and administered to the students before instruction begins. Anyone demonstrating the desired level of competency in the objectives will receive credit for them and doesn't need instruction. Students needing instruction will receive it, followed by testing of their competency in the objectives. These steps will be repeated until the student has demonstrated the appropriate level of competency in the stated objective.

Some teachers object to competency-based instruction, arguing that it teaches only for the test, that objectives cannot be articulated in demonstrable terms, that stated objectives are too confining and allow no latitude for spontaneous instruction. Others object to students' being able to obtain credit without receiving instruction.

Competency-based education causes all teachers to reconsider their theory of education. Should students have to put in time in class or should they get credit for what they know, no matter where or how it was learned? Are teachers willing to put down in black and white exactly what they expect students to learn and are they then willing to stand by that? Are teachers willing to teach a topic until the students master it, or to omit a beloved lesson if no one needs it?

23. Teachers' objections to competency-based education may include all of the following except:

    (A) Students receive credit without instruction.
    (B) It is difficult to write down the component parts of the learning unit.
    (C) It allows for too much variation in teaching.
    (D) There is too much pre- and post-testing involved.

24. One can say that competency-based education is

    (A) a brand-new concept
    (B) a concept that has been used continuously in American education
    (C) an idea imported from European schools
    (D) similar to the method of earning badges in the Girl Scouts and the Boy Scouts

25. What changes can be anticipated where competency-based education is implemented?

    (A) no noticeable change
    (B) a diversity in the relative progress of the students
    (C) many objections from teachers
    (D) a greater diversity in teaching

26. An advantage of competency-based instruction is

    (A) that teachers do not have to confer with others teaching the same thing
    (B) that teachers have greater latitude in grading students
    (C) that teachers are more interested in their work
    (D) that students know what is expected of them

27. More than four million college students will own microcomputers by 1987. From 1982 to 1983, the number of students who owned microcomputers tripled. By 1987 colleges will own another half million computers. Elementary and secondary schools are also ordering an astonishing number of computers. We can conclude that by 1987

    (A) every student will have a computer
    (B) there will be changes in who uses computers
    (C) computers will have turned out to be a fad

28. To address the problem of the lack of leaders in the field of continuing education, a program has been started to prepare administrators and faculty for the field. It will include an exchange program. Do you think this will be effective?

    (A) Yes, such programs have been shown to be effective.
    (B) No, such programs have been shown to be ineffective.
    (C) It will depend on how it is viewed by the participants.

29. Education is an integral part of the culture of every society. It has been shaped by existing _____, which it in turn helps to preserve and transmit.

    (A) people
    (B) customs
    (C) children

30. In educational research, positive correlation ranges between

    (A) 0 and 1
    (B) 0 and −1
    (C) 0 and 100

31. Experimentation, questionnaires, case studies, statistics, anecdotal records and tests are methods of research in education. Which is most practically used in a classroom?

    (A) experimentation
    (B) questionnaires
    (C) case studies
    (D) tests

32. Which of the following problems concern teachers?

    I. problems of behavior
    II. problems of learning
    III. problems of individual differences

    (A) I
    (B) I and II
    (C) I, II and III
    (D) I and III
    (E) II and III

33. Does heredity or environment have more influence on a person?

    (A) heredity
    (B) environment
    (C) both have influence

34. Which of the following are inherited characteristics?

    I. eye color
    II. accent
    III. potential height
    IV. lefthandedness

    (A) I and III
    (B) I, III and IV
    (C) I, II, III and IV
    (D) I, II, and IV

35. Children generally learn certain things in a certain order. Put the following stages of learning in chronological order.

    I. has reflex actions and responds to single objects
    II. learns to classify objects and apply logical reasoning
    III. emphasizes theory, generalization and abstraction

    (A) I, II, III
    (B) II, I, III
    (C) I, III, II
    (D) III, I, II

36. Normal adolescence is characterized by all of the following except

    (A) questioning
    (B) delinquency
    (C) imitation
    (D) impulsiveness

37. The ability to learn increases rapidly from birth, reaches its peak at the age of _____ and then declines very slowly.

    (A) 1
    (B) 5
    (C) 10
    (D) 20

38. In order to learn both mental and physical tasks, training and maturation (readiness) are important. Which is the determining factor in learning?

    (A) maturation
    (B) training
    (C) both equally

39. To foster creativity in children, a teacher should

    (A) have firm control of the class
    (B) be encouraging but maintain discipline
    (C) be encouraging and let ideas flow

40. A second grader will be more apt to learn about the street pattern in his neighborhood by

    (A) being told about it
    (B) making a map of it

41. Children's emotions are very important to learning. All of the following may lead to increased interest and activity except

    (A) sorrow
    (B) anger
    (C) joy

42. Learning is

    (A) an active process
    (B) a passive absorption of knowledge

43. The most effective external motivation for learning is

    (A) rivalry
    (B) reprimanding
    (C) praise
    (D) reward

44. A student is more apt to learn if she is

    (A) motivated by praise
    (B) motivated from within

45. The more senses that are involved, the faster the learning.

    (A) true
    (B) false

46. For first graders to learn,

    (A) activities and methods should be changed frequently
    (B) the same activity should be extended over a lengthy period

47. A child develops best in an environment of

    (A) stimulation from outside sources
    (B) calmness and austerity

48. Programmed learning (self-teaching devices) yields the best results when used for

    (A) introduction of new material
    (B) drill, such as multiplication tables and spelling

49. An advantage of programmed learning is that

    (A) each student can work at his own pace
    (B) all students work at the same pace

50. Good tests

    I. are accurate
    II. measure what they are intended to measure
    III. fill a need

    (A) I
    (B) II
    (C) III
    (D) II and III
    (E) I, II and III

51. Intelligence is

    (A) easy to measure because measurements have been refined and are accurate
    (B) difficult to measure because there is no accurate scale

52. Tests can be used for the purpose(s) of

    I. diagnosis
    II. motivation
    III. grouping students

    (A) I
    (B) II
    (C) III
    (D) II and III
    (E) I, II and III

53. In an experiment in which teachers were told that a group of their students tested above average,

    (A) the teachers treated differently those students with higher expectations, and the students' performance increased
    (B) the teachers treated differently those students with higher expectations, and there was no change in the students' performance
    (C) the teachers did not change their treatment of the students, and there was no change in the students' performance

54. Testing can tell everything about a student's abilities.

    (A) true
    (B) false

55. A fourth-grade teacher gave an arithmetic test to her students and found that they did not know how to multiply by two digits. She then prepared to teach this concept to the students. In this case the test was used for

    (A) diagnosis
    (B) achievement
    (C) classification

56. Diagnostic tests, followed by _____ instruction, help prevent _____ .

    (A) creative, failure
    (B) creative, bad habits
    (C) remedial, failure

57. An advantage of asking a test question that requires a specific answer is

    (A) the ease of grading
    (B) that it encourages creativeness
    (C) that it checks on memorization

58. A disadvantage of a free-response question, like an essay question, is that

    (A) the grading is subjective
    (B) students need to reason and make judgments
    (C) it can't be graded

59. If a student is repeatedly tardy, the appropriate punishment would be

    (A) suspension
    (B) double homework
    (C) detention

60. To promote a positive self-image in a student who thinks she can't do anything, the teacher could

    (A) give her tasks at which she can succeed and praise her for them
    (B) praise her for anything she does
    (C) praise her for her prettiness and the dress she is wearing

61. A teacher who wants to get the whole class involved in a lesson would use

    (A) a group lesson plan
    (B) individual lesson plans

62. The person responsible for classroom discipline is

    (A) the teacher
    (B) the principal
    (C) the superintendent
    (D) the school board

63. A teacher presenting a unit about an American holiday who wants to involve her multicultural class would

    (A) tell them of the importance of this holiday
    (B) ask the students how they celebrate this or a similar holiday
    (C) tell the students that this holiday replaces the holiday they currently celebrate

64. Which seating arrangement would be best for small group discussions?

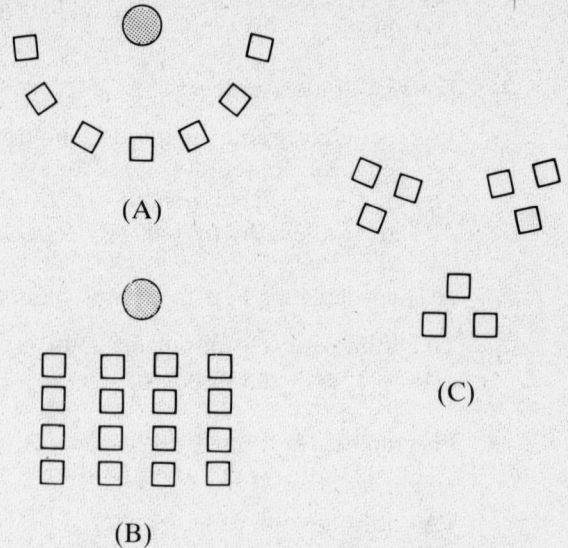

(A)

(B)

(C)

65. One reader for the third grade features a family in which the father is a lawyer. What effect can this have on a child whose family is receiving assistance?

    (A) encouragement to achieve
    (B) poor self-image
    (C) broadening of his realization of different lifestyles

66. A fifth-grade teacher is planning the introduction of a unit on careers. What would be most interesting to the class?

    (A) booklets on various careers
    (B) posters of people having different careers
    (C) people with different careers speaking and answering students' questions

67. On the local level, the _____ is responsible for educational policy and the _____ is responsible for implementation.

    (A) school board, school board
    (B) school board, superintendent
    (C) superintendent, school board
    (D) superintendent, superintendent

68. The Scopes trial of 1925 dealt with an educational controversy that has not yet been resolved. That controversy concerns

    (A) integration
    (B) school prayer
    (C) evolution

69. A teacher seeking to update his knowledge of current issues in his field of education would

    (A) enroll in a class at a teaching university
    (B) enroll in a class at a community college
    (C) attend an educational conference in his field

70. The main source of revenue for education is

    (A) state funding
    (B) federal funding
    (C) property taxes

    (D) sales tax
    (E) lotteries

71. Whether to promote a child to the next grade or not is a decision to be made by

    (A) the teacher
    (B) the principal
    (C) the parents
    (D) the teacher and parents

72. *Objectives* is the term used for

    (A) instructional results
    (B) instructional methods
    (C) teaching components
    (D) instructional assessment

73. When a teacher gives both a pre-test and a post-test with a unit, to insure validity

    (A) the questions should be different
    (B) the questions should be the same

ANSWERS TO SAMPLE TEST 2

BASIC SKILLS

Reading

1. C	11. E	21. C	31. B	41. A
2. E	12. E	22. E	32. C	42. D
3. D	13. A	23. C	33. D	43. A
4. D	14. C	24. A	34. D	44. C
5. B	15. A	25. A	35. C	45. D
6. D	16. E	26. E	36. C	46. B
7. C	17. C	27. B	37. A	47. A
8. E	18. B	28. D	38. B	48. B
9. C	19. A	29. B	39. D	49. C
10. B	20. C	30. C	40. C	50. C

Mathematics

1. B	11. A	21. D	31. C	41. D
2. A	12. A	22. A	32. D	42. B
3. D	13. A	23. C	33. C	43. C
4. B	14. B	24. B	34. B	44. C
5. D	15. B	25. C	35. B	45. A
6. A	16. A	26. B	36. C	46. C
7. C	17. C	27. D	37. A	47. D
8. C	18. A	28. D	38. D	48. C
9. D	19. C	29. D	39. A	49. B
10. B	20. D	30. B	40. B	50. D

Grammar

1. B	11. B	21. B	31. C	41. B
2. B	12. C	22. B	32. C	42. C
3. D	13. C	23. B	33. A	43. B
4. B	14. C	24. B	34. A	44. B
5. B	15. A	25. A	35. D	45. C
6. D	16. B	26. C	36. B	46. A
7. D	17. C	27. C	37. A	47. D
8. D	18. B	28. D	38. D	48. B
9. B	19. B	29. B	39. D	49. C
10. B	20. B	30. B	40. A	50. A

PROFESSIONAL KNOWLEDGE

1. A	16. D	31. D	46. A	61. A
2. D	17. B	32. C	47. A	62. A
3. D	18. B	33. C	48. B	63. B
4. B	19. C	34. B	49. A	64. C
5. A	20. A	35. A	50. E	65. B
6. D	21. A	36. B	51. B	66. C
7. D	22. D	37. D	52. E	67. B
8. D	23. C	38. A	53. A	68. C
9. A	24. D	39. B	54. B	69. C
10. B	25. B	40. B	55. A	70. C
11. D	26. D	41. A	56. C	71. D
12. C	27. B	42. A	57. A	72. A
13. C	28. C	43. C	58. A	73. B
14. A	29. B	44. B	59. C	
15. D	30. A	45. A	60. A	

EXPLANATION OF ANSWERS TO SAMPLE TEST 2

BASIC SKILLS

READING

1. **C** *Carnivorous* means *meat-eating*. Dogs, bears and cats are carnivorous.

2. **E** *But* means *only* or *merely* in this sentence.

3. **D** The person would keep working.

4. **D** The students are free to choose the courses outside their majors.

5. **B** Things are not being done in one big group.

6. **D**

County	Size	Population
Sussex	largest	smallest
Kent	middle	middle
New Castle	smallest	largest

7. **C**

8. **E** If you can walk anywhere, the bay must be shallow.

9. **C** *Earthbound* means *held to the earth*.

10. **B** A handicap is a disadvantage.

11. **E** A majority of anything is more than half.

12. **E** Nothing indicates what "it" is.

13. **A** The opposite of of southwest is northeast.

14. **C** Most of an iceberg is unseen and unknown, and walruses are the same.

15. **A** To bisect is to cut into two equal parts.

16. **E** The first and last sentence support the choice of E.

17. **C** The second sentence supports C.

18. **B** *Tri* in *triumvirate* means *three*.

19. **A** Study has been done, but we don't have all the answers yet.

20. **C** Use elimination to get the answer.

21. **C** Only 0.5% success rate is too small for diets to be considered generally successful.

22. **E** Lewis Carroll was the "author-artist."

23. **C** In this sentence *but* means *only*.

24. **A** "Who could have imagined" is a clue to the correct answer.

25. **A** A new problem has been created.

26. **E** The pollutants have to be expelled from the house, and ventilation accomplishes this.

27. **B** The drop is greater than the increase. Although there will likely be changes, that cannot be assumed from the passage.

28. **D**

29. **B** *Nemesis* means *downfall;* the sentence means that age has both benefits and detriments.

30. **C** Sentence 1 is verifiable. If there are many more lawyers, each one will probably have less business, but predictions of the future are opinions, not fact.

31. **B** Predictions of the future are speculation.

32. **C** Sentence 1 is fact. The others are based on supposition.

33–35. The best order of the sentences is 7, 1, 4, 8, 9, 2, 6, 3, 5.

33. **D**

34. **D**

35. **C**

36. **C**

37. **A**

38. **B**

39. **D**

40. **C**

41. **A** *Majestic* comes after *mailer.*

42. **D** *Clunk* comes after *clung.*

43. **A** *Rivulet* comes after *riviera.*

44. **C** *Stature* comes before *status.*

45. **D** *Loose* comes before *lose.*

46. **B** In general, write out each word to see which looks right. Emancipated

47. **A** regardless

48. **B** slippage

49. **C** skillful

50. **C** Irresistible

MATHEMATICS

1. **B** Write the numbers in a column with the decimals lined up. As soon as you find that the answer is a whole number, mark B.

2. **A** Check your addition carefully.

3. **D** The average has to be between 71 and 74.

4. **B** $\dfrac{1 \text{ in.}}{i} = \dfrac{2.54 \text{ cm}}{7 \text{ cm}}$

   Cross-multiply: $1 \times 7 = 2.54 \times i$

   $\dfrac{7}{2.54} = i$

   The answer has to be about 2½.

5. **D** $\dfrac{56}{7} = 8$ $8 \times \$1.26 = \$10.08$

6. **A** 1 square meter = 100 cm $\times$ 100 cm
   = 10,000 cm

   3 square meters = 3 $\times$ 10,000 cm
   = 30,000 square cm

7. **C** Estimate: 59.8 is near 60
   0.97 is near 1
   60 $\times$ 1 = 60; Eliminate
   A and D.

   Now multiply it out.

8. **C** Cancel: $\dfrac{\overset{1}{\cancel{3}}}{\underset{2}{\cancel{8}}} \times \dfrac{\overset{1}{\cancel{4}}}{\underset{3}{\cancel{21}}} = \dfrac{1}{6}$

9. **D** $\dfrac{7}{8} + \dfrac{2}{3} = \dfrac{7 \times 3}{8 \times 3} + \dfrac{2 \times 8}{3 \times 8} = \dfrac{21}{24} + \dfrac{16}{24} = \dfrac{37}{24} = 1\dfrac{13}{24}$

10. **B** $\dfrac{5}{6} - \dfrac{1}{4} = \dfrac{5 \times 2}{6 \times 2} - \dfrac{1 \times 3}{4 \times 3} - \dfrac{10 - 3}{12} = \dfrac{7}{12}$

11. **A** $\$\ .69$
    $.73$
    $.58$
    $.64$
    ___
    $\$\ 2.64$ $\$2.64 \div 4 = \$.66$

12. **A** The question asks for less than 45 degrees, so don't count day 2.

13. **A** From 9 am to 4 pm is 7 hours. The minutes make it just under 7 hours.

14. **B**

	4 gal	2 qt	1 pt	6 oz
			x	3
	12 gal	6 qt	3 pt	18 oz
16 oz = 1 pt	12 gal	6 qt	4 pt	2 oz
2 pt = 1 qt	12 gal	8 qt		2 oz
4 qt = 1 gal	14 gal			2 oz

15. **B** $4 \times$ side = perimeter
    $4s = 64$
    $s = 16$

16. **A** decimal $\times$ 100 = percent
    $0.068 \times 100 = 6.8\%$

17. **C** Start with   4 gal 2 qt 1 pt 6 oz
    borrow (1 pt = 16 oz)   4 gal 2 qt   22 oz
    $\underline{-3 \text{ gal 2 qt 1 pt } 7 \text{ oz}}$
                                                           15 oz
    borrow (1 qt = 2 pt)   4 gal 1 qt 2 pt
    $\underline{-3 \text{ gal 2 qt 1 pt}}$
                                             1 pt 15 oz
    borrow (1 gal = 4 qt)   3 gal 5 qt
    $\underline{-3 \text{gal 2 qt}}$
                                          3 qt 1 pt 15 oz

18. **A** Perimeter is 2 × length + 2 × width
$$2 × 4 + 2 × 6 = 20 \text{ ft}$$

19. **C** Add the digits: $1 + 6 + 7 + 5 + 2 = 21$
$$21 ÷ 3 = 7, \text{ no remainder}$$

20. **D** $\frac{2}{3} + \frac{3}{4} = \frac{2 × 4}{3 × 4} + \frac{3 × 3}{4 × 3} = \frac{8 + 9}{12} = \frac{17}{12}$

21. **D** $\frac{49}{56} ÷ \frac{7}{7} = \frac{7}{8}$

22. **A** $7)\overline{0.0847}$ gives 0.0121. Remember that the decimal stays in the same place.

23. **C** $5)\overline{4.00}$ gives 0.80

24. **B**
$$\begin{array}{r} \$5.75 \\ 27 × \$.35 = 9.45 \\ \hline \$15.20 \end{array}$$

25. **C** ⅛ × 100 = 12.5%

26. **B**
others	33%	
	17%	100%
	+ 25%	− 75%
	75%	Jeff 25% = ¼
		+ Jim 25% = ¼
		½

27. **D** $0.25)\overline{100}$
Move the decimal 2 places to the right in both numbers.
$$25)\overline{10,000} = 400$$

28. **D** $0.56 = \frac{56}{100} = \frac{14}{25}$

29. **D** $20)\overline{9.00}$ gives 0.45

30. **B** Reduce each answer: A $\frac{9 ÷ 9}{63 ÷ 9} = \frac{1}{7}$
B $\frac{42 ÷ 6}{54 ÷ 6} = \frac{7}{9}$

31. **C**
Th	F	M	T	W	Th	F
	1	2	3	4		
	Delivery			Delivery		

32. **D** Work with the last digit.
$12 ÷ 6 = 2$ No answer choice ends with 2.
$42 ÷ 6 = 7$ The answer is 477.

33. **C** $1.85 × 100 = 185\%$

34. **B** Add the last digits. $2 + 8 + 6 + 2 + 5 = 3$ Eliminate A and C. Add the numbers up to the hundreds column to find out whether the answer is 61,723 or 61,623.

35. **B**
$$\begin{array}{r} 7295 \text{ kwh} \\ - 7064 \text{ kwh} \\ \hline 231 \text{ kwh} \end{array}$$

36. **C** Eliminate B.
$$\begin{array}{r} 47.0800 \\ 9.0230 \\ 6.9710 \\ 0.0076 \\ 2.1050 \\ \hline 65.1866 \text{ inches} \end{array}$$

37. **A**
Original value
Depreciation 3 × $1,271.47
$$\begin{array}{r} \$8,799.00 \\ -3,814.41 \\ \hline \$4,984.59 \end{array}$$

38. **D**
$$\begin{array}{r} \$14.50 \\ -11.60 \\ \hline \$ 2.90 \end{array} \text{ or } \begin{array}{r} \$14.50 \\ × .20 \\ \hline \$2.9000 \end{array}$$

39. **A**
$$\begin{array}{r} 80,682 \\ -49,893 \\ \hline 30,789 \end{array}$$

40. **B** $6\frac{3}{10} = 6\frac{3 × 8}{10 × 8} = 6\frac{24}{80} = 5\frac{104}{80}$
$3\frac{9}{16} = 3\frac{9 × 5}{16 × 5} = 3\frac{45}{80} = 3\frac{45}{80} =$
$5\frac{104}{80} - 3\frac{45}{80} = 2\frac{59}{80}$

41. **D** *Product* means multiply.
$$\begin{array}{r} 176 \\ × 28 \\ \hline 1,408 \\ 352 \\ \hline 4,928 \end{array}$$

42. **B**
$$\begin{array}{r} 5,008 \\ × 79 \\ \hline 45,072 \\ 35,056 \\ \hline 395,632 \end{array}$$

43. **C** $0.725 \times 100 = 72.5\%$

44. **C** The only year when the average teacher's salary was less than the cost of living was 1981.

45. **A** Use the edge of your answer sheet to line it up.

46. **C**

47. **D** Area is length × width.
$$24 \text{ cm} \times 17 \text{ cm} = 408 \text{ cm}^2$$

48. **C** Sharon will withdraw more than she deposits. Eliminate A and B.

Total she is able to withdraw: principal + interest
Interest = principal × rate of interest × time (years)

$I = P \times R \times T$
$I = 4,000 \times 6/100 \times 5 = \$1,200$
$P = \underline{4,000}$
Total at withdrawal $\$5,200$

49. **B** He worked more than 40 hours. Eliminate A.

	hr	min
Regular	40	00
Mon.	3	29
Tues.	2	43
Wed.	1	56
Thurs.	1	37
	47 hr	165 min = 49 hr 45 min

50. **D** Area of square = side × side =
$$29 \times 29 = 841 \text{ sq in.}$$

GRAMMAR

1. **B** Add each breakfast and dinner.

2. **B** receipt

3. **D** *The Rise and Fall of Rio*

4. **B** Either (one) seems excellent. Or, "Both seem excellent."

5. **B** Jerry could hardly stop laughing. *Hardly* is a negative word. You don't need another one.

6. **D** They earn the same where the lines cross.

7. **D** handkerchief

8. **D** On Wednesday Sally and I saw the birds flying south (direction) for the winter (season).

9. **B** Neither Horace nor Harry wanted the job, since it meant relocating. Neither . . . nor.

10. **B** It's (it is) your birthday!

11. **B** *Effect* is the more common choice when you need a noun. As a verb it means "to bring about."

12. **C** Rent 32%; food 30%; clothing, transportation and entertainment 33%, clothing and other 23%.

13. **C** Martha was able to complete the report with the help of her many assistants.

14. **C** As a subject area, *physics* is not capitalized. A course title, such as Physics II, would be capitalized.

15. **A** The author compares Harry with Sheila.

16. **B**

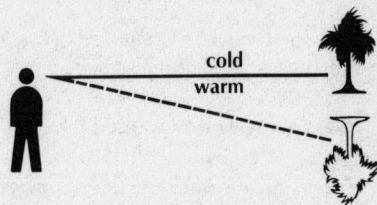

17. **C** *vane*–an indicator, usually of wind
vein–a blood vessel
vain–unusually proud of oneself

18. **B** Lawrence told Doctor Jones that he wanted to become a doctor.

19. **B** Bernie acts as though he were already the vice-principal.
The subjunctive is used when you suppose something that in reality isn't so.

20. **B** there–in that place
their–belonging to them
they're–contraction of *they are*

21. **B** The northeastern part of the state is mountainous.

22. **B** I didn't know to whom he was speaking. *Whom* is the object of *to.*

23. **B** *This* is singular; *these* is plural.

24. **B** He drank his orange juice every morning.

25. **A** The book was given to both you and me. Mention the other person before yourself. To decide whether to use *me* or *I*, say the sentence without the *you and*. The book was given to me.

26. **C** some

27. **C** *Stationery* is what you write on. *Stationary* is staying in one place.

28. **D** She had broken her engagement to him.

29. **B** Mr. Bradley likes (you and) him.

30. **B** *Viscosity* is the thickness of a semiliquid like oil.

31. **C** *Urban* refers to city; *rural* refers to country.

32. **C** *The Reader's Guide to Periodical Literature* lists articles from magazines. This is what you would consult to find the most recent articles.

33. **A** Use *most happy* or *happiest*. *Most happiest* is too much of a good thing.

34. **A** Every (single) boy wanted his own watch.

35. **D** *Except* means *but; accept* means *receive*.

36. **B** The sidewalks were already melting as the sun rose like a fireball out of the east.

37. **A** He was beside himself with worry. *Besides* means *also*.

38. **D** *Trepidation* is similar to *fear*.

39. **D** Who had stolen Mrs. Evertrue's necklace?

40. **A** A (one group) group (of boys) was waiting at the door, ready for lunch.

41. **B** *Horizontal* means in a flat position, while *vertical* means in an upright position.

42. **C** To recall is to remember.

43. **B** A simile uses *like* or *as*. Ed is *like* a meek lamb. A metaphor speaks of the person or object as though it were actually something else. Ed *is* a meek lamb.

44. **B** The passage goes into great detail.

45. **C** Statistics on rainfall in the U.S. would be found in *The Farmer's Almanac*, but to find Peru's rainfall you need an encyclopedia.

46. **A** A simile uses *like* or *as*.

47. **D** It discusses increased enrollment specifically in teacher education programs.

48. **B** Louis *was* a volcano.

49. **C** *Urbane* means *sophisticated*. An urbane person is not necessarily witty.

50. **A** White *as* a sheet.

PROFESSIONAL KNOWLEDGE

1. **A** The primary funding source exerts the greatest influence.

2. **D** Showing how something can be of immediate use is the best reinforcement of learning.

3. **D** The colleges will consider all of the actions, then act upon those they think best.

4. **B** Children know when praise is deserved.

5. **A** The teacher's enthusiasm is what sparks students' interest and learning.

6. **D** Start by letting students read what they want, and they will gradually improve their level of reading.

7. **D** All the choices are possible and would affect schools. If women have fewer children, fewer schools will be needed. If these mothers are more affluent, they will have a greater choice of schools. If the mothers are employed, day care will be an important issue.

8. **D** What teachers do affects students, even if it is outside the classroom.

9. **A** The more formal the dress, the better the discipline.

10. **B** See answer 9.

11. **D** See answer 9.

12. **C** Red is irritating to students; therefore, use another color.

13. **C** Students will be motivated when they know what they are trying to achieve. The teacher must know what he or she is aiming for.

14. **A** As a role model he will need to lead a circumspect life.

15. **D** The statement is against extremes.

16. **D** The students are looking for job skills. No other answer makes sense.

17. **B** A reflexive question mirrors what the speaker said.

18. **B** "Children who are listened to are likely to be better behaved" leads to this conclusion.

19. **C** A woman with a bachelor's degree will earn up to $523,000, while a man with a high-school diploma will earn $861,000.

20. **A** The teachers will have the same amount of work to do on both schedules.

21. **A** All of the others are mentioned in the paragraph.

22. **D** Explaining theory to a third-grade class is not worthwhile.

23. **C** Competency-based education does not allow much variation in teaching, as objectives are very specific.

24. **D** If a student can do the work, he gets the credit, just as a Boy Scout gets the badge if he can do the task.

25. **B** The students will progress at their own rates and will diversify.

26. **D** The teacher and students know what is expected.

27. **B** Computer use is rapidly changing.

28. **C** If the consumers value the program, it will be effective.

29. **B** Customs transmit culture.

30. **A** Negative correlation is −1 to 0; positive correlation is 0 to 1.

31. **D** The other three alternatives are not appropriate for classroom use.

32. **C** All the problems concern teachers.

33. **C** Both heredity and environment shape a person.

34. **B** Eye color, potential height and handedness are inherited; accent is acquired from the environment.

35. **A** I. birth to two years
    II. early and late childhood
   III. adolescence and maturity

36. **B** Delinquency is not considered normal.

37. **D** College age is the peak learning time.

38. **A** A child can be taught, but unless he is ready to absorb the information, he will not learn.

39. **B** Children cannot learn in a chaotic environment. Creativity needs to be encouraged in a structured way.

40. **B** The more realistic a setting for learning is, the more readily the student will learn.

41. **A** Sorrow has the most debilitating effect on learning.

42. **A** Learning is an active process. The sponge theory is the least effective learning method.

43. **C** Praise is the most effective external motivation for learning.

44. **B** Self-motivation is best.

45. **A** Each sense adds to learning.

46. **A** First graders have a short attention span.

47. **A** Stimulation is essential to learning.

48. **B** Programmed learning is excellent for drill. If the student knows the material, he progresses rapidly. If he needs review, that is furnished.

49. **A** Programmed learning is self-paced.

50. **E** Good tests meet all three criteria.

51. **B** Intelligence has innumerable facets.

52. **E** Tests can be used for all three purposes. It is important that the tests reflect a purpose and that the students know the purpose.

53. **A** Students live up to what is expected of them. Teachers expect students to perform according to what they are told.

54. **B** Testing can inform us only about the student's knowledge that day on that question.

55. **A** The teacher diagnosed the students' need for instruction. Had they all passed the test, she would not have needed to teach the concept.

56. **C** Diagnostic tests, followed by remedial instruction, help prevent failure.

57. **A** Specific answers make grading of tests easier.

58. **A** Free-response questions require the teacher to make subjective judgments when grading.

59. **C** The student needs to learn that he is to spend a certain number of hours in school.

60. **A** Help the student to succeed. A student can tell whether praise is genuine or not.

61. **A** The whole group (class) would be involved.

62. **A** The teacher is responsible for discipline in the classroom.

63. **B** Making the students feed good about their culture and sharing the information unifies the class.

64. **C** C shows small groups.

65. **B** The students think that the textbooks reflect the ideal family. If that is drastically different from their own, it can cause a poor self-image.

66. **C** People who can answer questions are more interesting than books or posters.

67. **B** The school board sets policy, which the superintendent is responsible for carrying out.

68. **C** The Scopes trial was about the teaching of evolution.

69. **C** Conferences usually present the latest information.

70. **C** Property taxes are the major source of revenue for schools.

71. **D** The teacher and parents should decide what is best for the child.

72. **A** An objective states what will happen and what the results will be.

73. **B** The same questions give the best validity. As soon as a question is changed, the test is changed, reducing validity.

SAMPLE TEST 3

Sample Test 3 is similar to the Florida test. You can also use this test to practice for tests given in Alabama, Colorado, Georgia, Nebraska, Oregon and South Carolina. The professional-knowledge portion can be used to prepare for any state that has a professional-knowledge component, such as Arizona and Alaska.

You have 45 minutes for the writing test. From the two topics offered, you must choose one as the subject for your essay. You have two hours for the Basic-Skills section, which includes both mathematics and reading tests. Distribute your time as you think best. The reading portion doesn't take very long, so I suggest you do that first, then the mathematics. You might use 50 minutes or less for the reading and 70 minutes for the mathematics. After a lunch break there is a two-and-a-half-hour professional-skills test.

No scratch paper is provided, so write on the test booklet. The number of answer choices varies from question to question. To be confident of passing the test, you should answer 64 reading questions, 40 mathematics questions and 64 professional-knowledge questions correctly.

WRITING
45 Minutes–One Essay

Directions: You have 45 minutes to write an essay on either Topic 1 or Topic 2. The essay topics are intended to measure how well you write, given limitations on time and subject matter. Quality is more important than quantity. Spend some of your time organizing your thoughts. Supporting statements and examples should be specific. Write only on the assigned topic. Write legibly and within the lines provided. Space for notes is provided below.

Topic 1
What is the most important thing you learned from student teaching, and in what way did it change your concept of teaching?

Topic 2
George Whitefield said, "I had rather wear out than rust out." Using your experience and observations, explain why you agree or disagree.

(Write "**Topic 1**" or "**Topic 2**")

_____

_____

_____

_____

_____

_____

_____

_____

_____

_____

_____

_____

_____

_____

_____

_____

_____

_____

_____

_____

ANSWER SHEETS FOR SAMPLE TEST 3

BASIC SKILLS

Mathematics

	A B C D E		A B C D E		A B C D E		A B C D E		A B C D E
1	○○○○○	11	○○○○○	21	○○○○○	31	○○○○○	41	○○○○○
2	○○○○○	12	○○○○○	22	○○○○○	32	○○○○○	42	○○○○○
3	○○○○○	13	○○○○○	23	○○○○○	33	○○○○○	43	○○○○○
4	○○○○○	14	○○○○○	24	○○○○○	34	○○○○○	44	○○○○○
5	○○○○○	15	○○○○○	25	○○○○○	35	○○○○○	45	○○○○○
6	○○○○○	16	○○○○○	26	○○○○○	36	○○○○○	46	○○○○○
7	○○○○○	17	○○○○○	27	○○○○○	37	○○○○○	47	○○○○○
8	○○○○○	18	○○○○○	28	○○○○○	38	○○○○○	48	○○○○○
9	○○○○○	19	○○○○○	29	○○○○○	39	○○○○○	49	○○○○○
10	○○○○○	20	○○○○○	30	○○○○○	40	○○○○○	50	○○○○○

Reading

	A B C D E		A B C D E		A B C D E		A B C D E		A B C D E
1	○○○○○	11	○○○○○	21	○○○○○	31	○○○○○	41	○○○○○
2	○○○○○	12	○○○○○	22	○○○○○	32	○○○○○	42	○○○○○
3	○○○○○	13	○○○○○	23	○○○○○	33	○○○○○	43	○○○○○
4	○○○○○	14	○○○○○	24	○○○○○	34	○○○○○	44	○○○○○
5	○○○○○	15	○○○○○	25	○○○○○	35	○○○○○	45	○○○○○
6	○○○○○	16	○○○○○	26	○○○○○	36	○○○○○	46	○○○○○
7	○○○○○	17	○○○○○	27	○○○○○	37	○○○○○	47	○○○○○
8	○○○○○	18	○○○○○	28	○○○○○	38	○○○○○	48	○○○○○
9	○○○○○	19	○○○○○	29	○○○○○	39	○○○○○	49	○○○○○
10	○○○○○	20	○○○○○	30	○○○○○	40	○○○○○	50	○○○○○

Reading (continued)

	A B C D E		A B C D E		A B C D E		A B C D E		A B C D E
51	○ ○ ○ ○ ○	57	○ ○ ○ ○ ○	63	○ ○ ○ ○ ○	69	○ ○ ○ ○ ○	75	○ ○ ○ ○ ○
52	○ ○ ○ ○ ○	58	○ ○ ○ ○ ○	64	○ ○ ○ ○ ○	70	○ ○ ○ ○ ○	76	○ ○ ○ ○ ○
53	○ ○ ○ ○ ○	59	○ ○ ○ ○ ○	65	○ ○ ○ ○ ○	71	○ ○ ○ ○ ○	77	○ ○ ○ ○ ○
54	○ ○ ○ ○ ○	60	○ ○ ○ ○ ○	66	○ ○ ○ ○ ○	72	○ ○ ○ ○ ○	78	○ ○ ○ ○ ○
55	○ ○ ○ ○ ○	61	○ ○ ○ ○ ○	67	○ ○ ○ ○ ○	73	○ ○ ○ ○ ○	79	○ ○ ○ ○ ○
56	○ ○ ○ ○ ○	62	○ ○ ○ ○ ○	68	○ ○ ○ ○ ○	74	○ ○ ○ ○ ○	80	○ ○ ○ ○ ○

PROFESSIONAL KNOWLEDGE

	A B C D E		A B C D E		A B C D E		A B C D E		A B C D E
1	○ ○ ○ ○ ○	17	○ ○ ○ ○ ○	33	○ ○ ○ ○ ○	49	○ ○ ○ ○ ○	65	○ ○ ○ ○ ○
2	○ ○ ○ ○ ○	18	○ ○ ○ ○ ○	34	○ ○ ○ ○ ○	50	○ ○ ○ ○ ○	66	○ ○ ○ ○ ○
3	○ ○ ○ ○ ○	19	○ ○ ○ ○ ○	35	○ ○ ○ ○ ○	51	○ ○ ○ ○ ○	67	○ ○ ○ ○ ○
4	○ ○ ○ ○ ○	20	○ ○ ○ ○ ○	36	○ ○ ○ ○ ○	52	○ ○ ○ ○ ○	68	○ ○ ○ ○ ○
5	○ ○ ○ ○ ○	21	○ ○ ○ ○ ○	37	○ ○ ○ ○ ○	53	○ ○ ○ ○ ○	69	○ ○ ○ ○ ○
6	○ ○ ○ ○ ○	22	○ ○ ○ ○ ○	38	○ ○ ○ ○ ○	54	○ ○ ○ ○ ○	70	○ ○ ○ ○ ○
7	○ ○ ○ ○ ○	23	○ ○ ○ ○ ○	39	○ ○ ○ ○ ○	55	○ ○ ○ ○ ○	71	○ ○ ○ ○ ○
8	○ ○ ○ ○ ○	24	○ ○ ○ ○ ○	40	○ ○ ○ ○ ○	56	○ ○ ○ ○ ○	72	○ ○ ○ ○ ○
9	○ ○ ○ ○ ○	25	○ ○ ○ ○ ○	41	○ ○ ○ ○ ○	57	○ ○ ○ ○ ○	73	○ ○ ○ ○ ○
10	○ ○ ○ ○ ○	26	○ ○ ○ ○ ○	42	○ ○ ○ ○ ○	58	○ ○ ○ ○ ○	74	○ ○ ○ ○ ○
11	○ ○ ○ ○ ○	27	○ ○ ○ ○ ○	43	○ ○ ○ ○ ○	59	○ ○ ○ ○ ○	75	○ ○ ○ ○ ○
12	○ ○ ○ ○ ○	28	○ ○ ○ ○ ○	44	○ ○ ○ ○ ○	60	○ ○ ○ ○ ○	76	○ ○ ○ ○ ○
13	○ ○ ○ ○ ○	29	○ ○ ○ ○ ○	45	○ ○ ○ ○ ○	61	○ ○ ○ ○ ○	77	○ ○ ○ ○ ○
14	○ ○ ○ ○ ○	30	○ ○ ○ ○ ○	46	○ ○ ○ ○ ○	62	○ ○ ○ ○ ○	78	○ ○ ○ ○ ○
15	○ ○ ○ ○ ○	31	○ ○ ○ ○ ○	47	○ ○ ○ ○ ○	63	○ ○ ○ ○ ○	79	○ ○ ○ ○ ○
16	○ ○ ○ ○ ○	32	○ ○ ○ ○ ○	48	○ ○ ○ ○ ○	64	○ ○ ○ ○ ○	80	○ ○ ○ ○ ○

120 Minutes–130 Questions

Directions: Choose the best answer for each question and blacken the corresponding space on the Answer Sheets for Sample Test 3. The correct answers and the explanations follow the test.

MATHEMATICS (50 Questions)

1. Beth and Kay drive separate cars from Stardust to Knightown, a distance of 300 miles. They both start at the same time. Beth drives at 60 miles per hour, while Kay drives at 50 miles per hour. Who will arrive in Knightown first, and by how much?

   (A) Beth by 1 hour
   (B) Kay by 1 hour
   (C) Beth by 5 hours
   (D) They will arrive at the same time.

2. Harry is editing a 180-page book. He edited one quarter of it the first week in May and another quarter of it the second week. He wants to divide the remaining pages evenly over the last two weeks of May. How many pages will he have to edit each of the last two weeks?

   (A) 15 pages
   (B) 45 pages
   (C) 26 pages
   (D) 90 pages

3. $-6 - (+9) =$

   (A) -3
   (B) 3
   (C) 15
   (D) -15

4. Kenny had a balance of $107.52 in his checking account. On Tuesday he wrote checks for $57.61 and $47.16. Wednesday he deposited his paycheck of $452.63. He got his statement from the bank showing service charges of $9.70 on Thursday. In order to balance his checkbook, Kenny should take his beginning balance of $107.52 and

   (A) add $452.63 and $9.70, subtract $57.61 and 47.16
   (B) add $452.63, $57.61 and $47.16, subtract $9.70
   (C) subtract $452.63, add $9.70, $57.61 and $47.16
   (D) add $452.63, subtract $57.61, $47.16 and $9.70

Questions 5 to 7

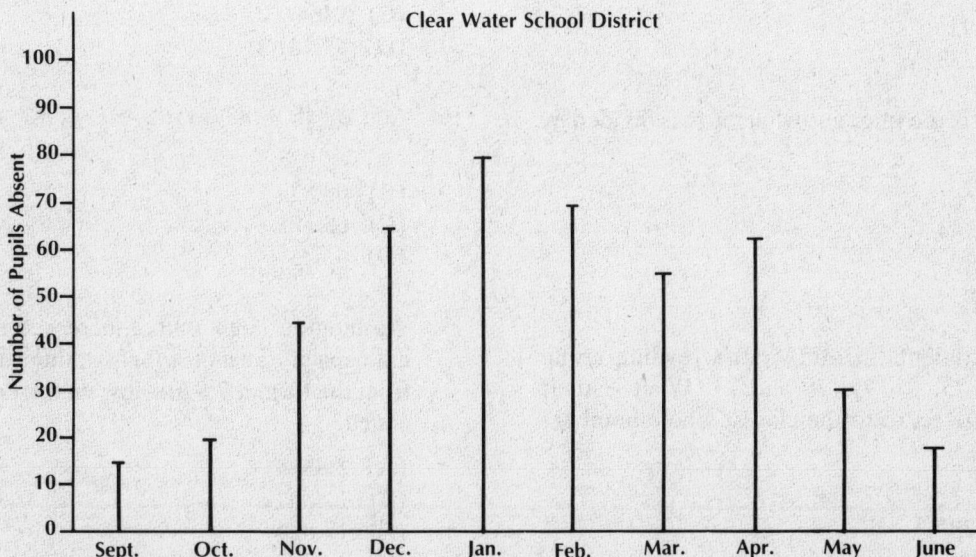

Clear Water School District

5. How many students were absent in December?

   (A) 80
   (B) 60
   (C) 65
   (D) 70

6. Approximately how many absences were there during the school year?

   (A) 450
   (B) 460
   (C) 470
   (D) 480

7. What was the approximate average number of absences each month?

   (A) 35
   (B) 40
   (C) 45
   (D) 50

8. Mr. Jeremy earns $18,408 a year. What is his monthly salary?

   (A) $1,840.80
   (B) $184,080
   (C) $1,534
   (D) $220,896

9. When 173,712 is divided by 231, what is the remainder?

   (A) 117
   (B) 0
   (C) 93
   (D) 233

10. What is the quotient when 5616 is divided by 39?

    (A) 5616
    (B) 144
    (C) 39
    (D) 0

11. The students in Mrs. Carr's reading group score 75, 81, 79, 78 and 73. What is their average score to the closest whole number?

    (A) 75
    (B) 77
    (C) 78
    (D) 79

12. Shona had monthly bank balances of $1,024.57, $1,246.85, $30.47, $117.61, $351.13, $573.37, $1994.55, $65.76, $1,708.84, $2,007.92, $3,462.01, $1,280.09. What was her average balance for the year?

    (A) $1,155.27
    (B) $1,155.26
    (C) $1,386.32
    (D) $13,863.17

13. How much more than 7 lb 7 oz is 11 lb 5 oz?

    (A) 3 lb 14 oz
    (B) 4 lb 2 oz
    (C) 3 lb 8 oz
    (D) 18 lb 12 oz

Questions 14 and 15

Thomas is carpeting his den, which measures 17 feet by 27 feet. The carpet he buys cost $9 per square yard.

14. How many square yards of carpet will he have to buy?

    (A) 45
    (B) 51
    (C) 54
    (D) 459

15. How much will the carpeting cost?

    (A) $405
    (B) $459
    (C) $486
    (D) $4,131

16. Add 2,745 + 839 + 62,487 + 987 + 1,247.

    (A) 68,035
    (B) 68,835
    (C) 68,305
    (D) 6,835

17. Washington High School increased the seating capacity at its football stadium to 9,850 from the former 7,970. How many seats were added?

    (A) 2,880
    (B) 1,880
    (C) 17,820
    (D) 1,820

18. A car has a 17-gallon gas tank. If it averages 29 miles per gallon, how far can it travel on a tank of gas?

    (A) 503 miles
    (B) 12 miles
    (C) 46 miles
    (D) 493 miles

19. Widget stock opened for the week at 17 $\frac{5}{8}$. The stock gained $\frac{1}{8}$ point on Monday, $\frac{7}{8}$ on Tuesday, $1\frac{1}{2}$ on Wednesday, $\frac{3}{4}$ on Thursday and $\frac{3}{8}$ on Friday. What was the closing quotation of Widget stock at the end of the week?

    (A) $3\frac{5}{8}$
    (B) $20\frac{10}{8}$
    (C) $20\frac{2}{8}$
    (D) $21\frac{1}{4}$

20. Jane bought a washing machine for $595. She paid $85 down and will pay the balance in 30 equal monthly installments. How much is each payment?

    (A) $30
    (B) $85
    (C) $17
    (D) $35

21. If a passenger flies 10,000 miles on Horizon Airlines, she will get a free trip. Suzanne flew 4,576 miles in January, 1,379 miles in February and 3,597 miles in March. How many miles will she need to fly in April to qualify for the free trip?

    (A) none, she has flown more than 10,000 miles already
    (B) 48 miles
    (C) 448 miles
    (D) 488 miles

22. 98 is 35% of what number?

    (A) 133
    (B) 343
    (C) 280
    (D) 350

23. $\frac{1}{2} - \frac{1}{3} =$

    (A) $-\frac{0}{1}$
    (B) $\frac{2}{5}$
    (C) $\frac{1}{5}$
    (D) $\frac{1}{6}$

24. Kenny has a balance of $107.52 in his checking account. On Tuesday he wrote checks for $57.61 and $47.16. Wednesday he deposited his paycheck of $452.63. He got his statement from the bank showing a service charge of $9.70 on Thursday. What is the new balance in Kenny's checking account?

    (A) $465.08
    (B) $655.22
    (C) $444.28
    (D) $445.68

25. To mail a package costs $.20 for the first ounce and $.17 for each additional ounce. How much does a package weigh that costs $2.24 to mail?

    (A) 11.2 oz
    (B) 10.3 oz
    (C) 13 oz
    (D) 13.18 oz

26.

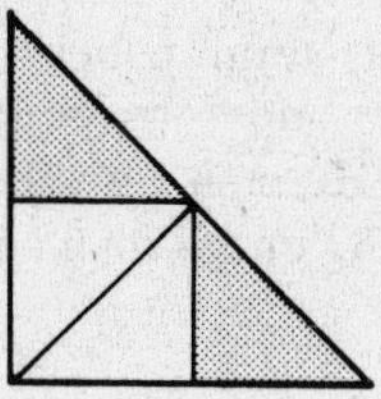

1

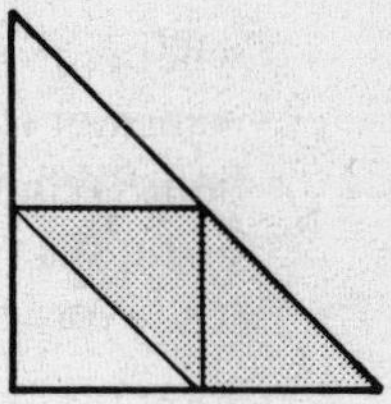

2

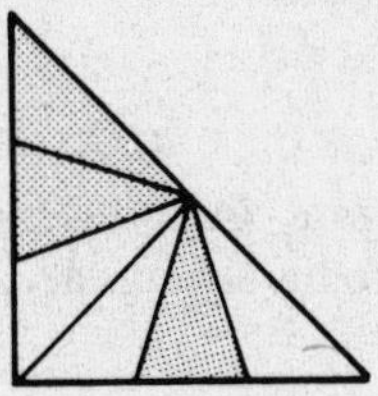

3

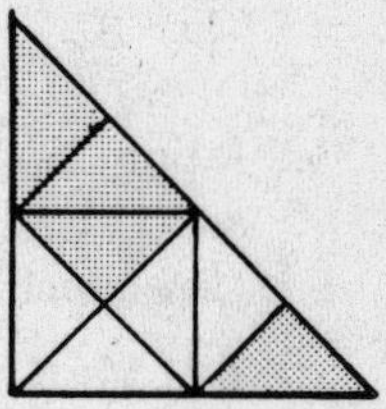

4

In which triangles are the shaded portions equivalent from one numbered triangle to the next?

    (A) none
    (B) 1 and 3
    (C) 1, 2 and 3
    (D) all

27. There was $\frac{5}{8}$ of a pie left over from dinner. Howard ate $\frac{2}{5}$ of what was left. How much of the pie did Howard eat?

(A) $\frac{1}{40}$
(B) $\frac{3}{8}$
(C) $\frac{1}{4}$
(D) $\frac{2}{3}$

28. Using the information from question 27, how much of the pie was left after Howard had his snack?

(A) $\frac{3}{8}$
(B) $\frac{1}{4}$
(C) $\frac{2}{3}$
(D) $\frac{1}{3}$

29. Find 0.375 of $28.65 to the nearest cent.

(A) $10.74
(B) $107.40
(C) $1,074.00
(D) $1,074,000.00

30. Mr. Friesen has worked out the following formula for year-end grades in history class:

$$\frac{(15\text{ P} + 67\text{ T} + 18\text{ F})}{100} = \text{final grade}$$

where P = grade on term paper; T = semester test average; and F = grade on final. What grade will Herman get if he had 74 on his term paper, 87 on his final and his test average was 69?

(A) 73
(B) 76
(C) 77
(D) 82

31. Ralph made deposits of $127.50, $1,547.05 and $57.55 to his savings account this month. How much did he add to his savings account?

(A) $1,740.10
(B) $1,732.10
(C) $1,732.05
(D) $1,740.05

32. The scale on a map is 1 inch = 30 miles. How far apart will two cities be on the map if the actual distance between them is 480 miles?

(A) 450 inches
(B) 510 inches
(C) 16 inches
(D) 16 miles

33. Harry is editing a 180-page book. He edited $\frac{1}{4}$ of it the first week in May and $\frac{1}{3}$ of the remainder the second week in May. He wants to divide the remaining pages to be edited evenly over the last two weeks of May. How many pages will he have to edit each of the last two weeks?

(A) 15 pages
(B) 26 pages
(C) 45 pages
(D) 60 pages

34. There are 34 students in each of three first grades. In the other three first grades there are 35, 37 and 31 students, respectively. How many first-grade students are in the school?

(A) 137
(B) 205
(C) 195
(D) 441

35. The expenses for the AB Company in March were $4,896.31. The gross income was $5,201.13. What was the net income?

(A) $305.22
(B) $304.82
(C) $304.22
(D) $305.18

36. Horace had a part-time job. Monday he worked $2\frac{3}{4}$ hours, Tuesday and Wednesday he worked $1\frac{1}{3}$ hours each, Thursday he worked $2\frac{1}{2}$ hours and on Friday he worked 3 hours. How many hours did he work last week?

(A) $10\frac{11}{12}$
(B) $9\frac{7}{12}$
(C) $9\frac{5}{12}$
(D) $9\frac{1}{3}$

37. Barbara bought the following items: hairspray, $2.97; cotton swabs, $1.39; cotton puffs, $1.27; shampoo, $2.57; hair rinse, $1.96; comb, $1.34. How much did she spend at the drug store?

(A) $11.60

(B) $11.45
(C) $11.50
(D) $11.40

38. Carole got 55% on her last test. The passing score is 70%. How much did she need to increase her score to pass?

(A) 125%
(B) 25%
(C) 15%
(D) 10%

39.

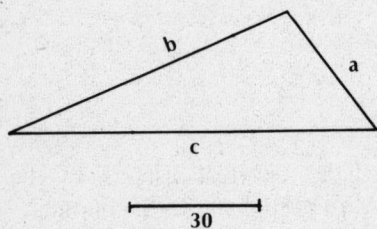

What is the length of side *b* according to the scale?

(A) 60
(B) 75
(C) 40
(D) 90

40. Mike bought a shirt for $12.96 and a tie for $8.77. He gave the clerk $25. How much change should he get?

(A) $3.27
(B) $12.04
(C) $16.23
(D) $21.73

41.

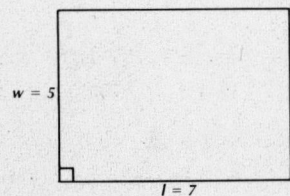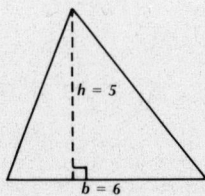

Irene wants to carpet two play areas. The formula for the area is given below each figure. What is the total area to be carpeted?

(A) 15
(B) 23
(C) 35
(D) 50

42. 7.12 [2.3 − (0.6 × 7 − 1.9)] =

(A) −27.056
(B) 0
(C) 10.276
(D) 26.9136

43. What is ½ of ⅓?

(A) −½
(B) ⅟₆₃
(C) ⅔₃
(D) ½

44. Clark bought a set of tires for $178.15. The tax rate is 6%. How much sales tax did he pay?

(A) $10.69
(B) $29.69
(C) $2.96
(D) $10.78

45. A teacher works seven hours a day for 186 days during the school year. Of that time, ⅔ is nonteaching time, and ⅟₁₅ of the nonteaching time is spent in meetings. How many hours are spent in meetings each year?

(A) 4⅔
(B) 24⅕
(C) 118
(D) 43

46. The Horatio Alger High School cafeteria serves 760 students. One hundred grams of meat is used in each hamburger. If each student gets two hamburgers, how many kilos of beef are used?

(A) 152
(B) 380
(C) 1520
(D) 15,200

47. Carole is making costumes for the school play. Each costume uses ⅝ yard of fabric. How many costumes can she make out of 7 ⅕ yards of fabric?

(A) ⁹⁄₁₂
(B) 11
(C) 25
(D) 288

48. Mr. Everett's monthly salary is $1,250, of which he saves $137.50. What percentage of his salary does he save?

(A) 0.11%
(B) 11%
(C) 11.25%
(D) 17.1875%

49. Elaine was born on November 12, 1978. How old was she when she started school on September 9, 1984?

(A) 6 years, 2 months, 3 days
(B) 5 years, 9 months, 3 days
(C) 5 years, 2 months, 27 days
(D) 5 years, 9 months, 27 days

50.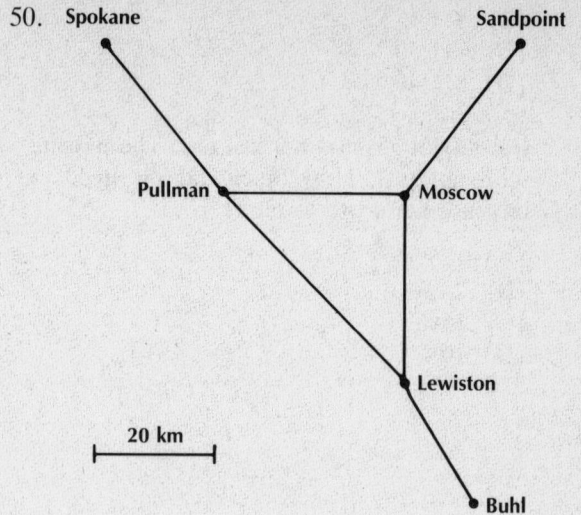

What is the shortest distance by the roads shown from Spokane to Sandpoint?

(A) 67 km
(B) 140 km
(C) 90 km
(D) 104 km

READING (80 Questions)

Directions: Choose the word that best fits into each blank in the passage.

Questions 1 to 10

One of the things that new teachers or _____
                                              1
in a new situation fear is losing control of the

_____. Letting a class have group discussion
    2

or break into _____ for an activity
                    3

_____ a certain _____ of abdication of
    4   5

control and trust in the group. Without this,

however, few teachers can _____ a high level
                                6

of _____ achievement. How this important
      7

facet of _____ is to be _____ is the
              8   9

subject of _____ discussion and debate.
                 10

1. (A) teachers
   (B) assistance
   (C) administrators
   (D) students

2. (A) discipline
   (B) reins
   (C) lesson
   (D) class

3. (A) groups
   (B) pieces
   (C) cliques
   (D) friends

4. (A) portends
   (B) involves
   (C) places
   (D) pretends

5. (A) total
   (B) limit
   (C) segment
   (D) amount

6. (A) attest
   (B) set
   (C) attain
   (D) get

7. (A) requirement
   (B) peak
   (C) goal
   (D) aim

8. (A) teaching
   (B) learning
   (C) student
   (D) teacher

9. (A) applied
   (B) approached
   (C) used
   (D) arranged

10. (A) angry
    (B) many
    (C) lengthy
    (D) considerable

Questions 11 to 20

Many teachers who _____ involvement say
                        11
that it makes a class more _____. It seems to
                                12
make the time go faster and make a class less

boring. It _____ students to concentrate on
                13
the _____. They can't "tune out." There
       14
_____ many other reasons given for involve-
     15
ment, but the only _____ that it should be
                         16
_____ is that it is the best method _____
     17   18
accomplishing the _____ learning goal. This
                       19
criterion should be used in deciding whether to

use any _____ technique.
             20

11. (A) avoid
     (B) advance
     (C) advocate
     (D) avow

12. (A) interesting
     (B) active
     (C) challenging
     (D) action

13. (A) makes
     (B) plods
     (C) coerces
     (D) forces

14. (A) book
     (B) subject
     (C) item
     (D) blackboard

15. (A) are
     (B) seem to be
     (C) were
     (D) will be

16. (A) reason
     (B) purpose
     (C) wary
     (D) method

17. (A) noticed
     (B) used
     (C) discarded
     (D) ignored

18. (A) for
     (B) to
     (C) of
     (D) how

19. (A) specific
     (B) corollary
     (C) momentous
     (D) specious

20. (A) learning
     (B) processed
     (C) training
     (D) teaching

Questions 21 to 30

Adults can learn from listening to _____ , but
                                        21
they are more likely to _____ from discus-
                             22
sion. Since nearly all _____ learning is self-
                            23
directed, why do some not _____ in discus-
                                24
sion? _____ questioning you will often find
          25
that the _____ thinks that she will be
              26
_____ and that her ideas are not _____
    27   28
to the group. This person has been trained not to
participate, and until this _____ is over-
                                 29
come, she will not get the full learning _____
                                              30
that she should from a teaching session.

21. (A) lectures
     (B) tapes
     (C) videos
     (D) discussion

22. (A) achieve
     (B) learn
     (C) advance
     (D) shy

23. (A) valuable
     (B) childhood
     (C) cogent
     (D) adult

24. (A) result
     (B) participate
     (C) recommend
     (D) advise

25. (A) Despite
     (B) Without
     (C) With
     (D) Upon

26. (A) nonparticipant
     (B) participant
     (C) advocate
     (D) instructor

27. (A) ostracized
    (B) deleted
    (C) embarrassed
    (D) challenged

28. (A) tolerated
    (B) viable
    (C) valuable
    (D) received

29. (A) feeling
    (B) idea
    (C) neuroticism
    (D) training

30. (A) benefits
    (B) idea
    (C) joys
    (D) training

Questions 31 to 40

A recent _____ revealed that college stu-
              31
dents don't think that their _____ should be
                              32
humorous. When questioned _____, they
                            33
said that professors who used _____ in the
                               34
classroom were not projecting the correct

_____, and did not seem to take themselves,
    35
the subject or the _____ seriously enough.
                    36
Interestingly though, students _____ the
                                37
serious material the professor using humor pre-

sented much _____ than the material of
              38
nonhumorous _____. Could it be that these
               39
students think that learning has to be _____?
                                        40

31. (A) book
    (B) survey
    (C) thesis
    (D) theory

32. (A) professors
    (B) friends

(C) parents
(D) counselors

33. (A) further
    (B) again
    (C) later
    (D) persistently

34. (A) charts
    (B) posters
    (C) humor
    (D) experiments

35. (A) image
    (B) position
    (C) posters
    (D) format

36. (A) university
    (B) department
    (C) peers
    (D) students

37. (A) remember
    (B) forget
    (C) like
    (D) enjoy

38. (A) less
    (B) better
    (C) slower
    (D) deeper

39. (A) people
    (B) lectures
    (C) professors
    (D) friends

40. (A) fun
    (B) humorous
    (C) serious
    (D) dull

Questions 41 to 50

Salesmen make a point of _____ your name
                          41
and using it often. Teachers are salesmen of sorts,

too. Think how _____ it feels when someone
                42
remembers your name, and how _____ it
                               43

feels when someone doesn't. It is _____ to
                        44

learn your students' names as soon as possible.

_____ each student as he comes into the
   45

room, _____ on his name and using it will
          46

help you remember. If the students keep the same

_____ you will more readily _____ the
  47   48

name and the face. Try to think of something

distinctive that will _____ the person's face
                         49

and name. The more often you use a person's

name, the better you will remember it. What did

you say your _____ is, again?
            50

41.   (A) saying
      (B) learning
      (C) speaking
      (D) reading

42.   (A) happy
      (B) new
      (C) good
      (D) novel

43.   (A) good
      (B) poor
      (C) strange
      (D) awful

44.   (A) important
      (B) convenient
      (C) pleasant
      (D) customary

45.   (A) Meeting
      (B) Greeting
      (C) Seeing
      (D) Watching

46.   (A) thinking
      (B) contemplating
      (C) concentrating
      (D) looking

47.   (A) names
      (B) friends
      (C) nametags
      (D) places

48.   (A) remember
      (B) recall
      (C) associate
      (D) forget

49.   (A) link
      (B) combine
      (C) stand out
      (D) erase

50.   (A) school
      (B) job
      (C) position
      (D) name

Questions 51 to 60

How you treat your _____ at an early age
                        51

may affect _____ he becomes a conformist
             52

or a (an) _____. Although _____ want
        53   54

their children to be well behaved and _____,
                            55

they want the children to grow up to be indepen-

tent and _____. _____ are influenced
          56   57

by their own situation. Parents belonging to lower

economic groups who want their children to

_____ will stress conformity as a way to get
   58

ahead. Parents who are secure in _____
                          59

society encourage their _____ to take risks.
                     60

51.   (A) pet
      (B) wife
      (C) husband
      (D) child

52.   (A) whether
      (B) how
      (C) if
      (D) when

53. (A) reprobate
    (B) individualist
    (C) delinquent
    (D) complaint

54. (A) teachers
    (B) parents
    (C) educators
    (D) impediments

55. (A) defenseless
    (B) tidy
    (C) compliant
    (D) complaint

56. (A) creative
    (B) dependent
    (C) quiet
    (D) unobtrusive

57. (A) Children
    (B) Girls
    (C) Boys
    (D) Parents

58. (A) conform
    (B) leave
    (C) succeed
    (D) stay

59. (A) established
    (B) primitive
    (C) edges
    (D) high

60. (A) friends
    (B) children
    (C) spouses
    (D) individuals

Questions 61 to 70

Teacher-education programs have come under much criticism lately. Many _____ advocate
                                              61
doing away with all teacher-education classes,

_____ courses on the material to be
62
_____. However, the teacher's knowledge of
63

_____ is of no value to the students
64
_____ the teacher can convey it to those
65
students. To do this, the teacher needs to learn about classroom control, grading, various methods of teaching to ensure maximum _____,
                                          66
how to make a lesson interesting and where and how to get _____ resources. The teacher also
                   67
needs to know about child and _____ psy-
                               68
chology, _____ law and the educational
         69
administrative system. Teacher-education courses are the best way to learn the tools of the

_____.
70

61. (A) professors
    (B) teachers
    (C) critics
    (D) students

62. (A) substituting
    (B) using
    (C) having
    (D) without

63. (A) used
    (B) new
    (C) learned
    (D) taught

64. (A) teaching
    (B) subject matter
    (C) facts
    (D) students

65. (A) unless
    (B) when
    (C) if
    (D) whether

66. (A) time
    (B) effort
    (C) lesson
    (D) learning

67. (A) appropriate
    (B) examination
    (C) college
    (D) school

68. (A) children
    (B) adult
    (C) school
    (D) adolescent

69. (A) state
    (B) civil rights
    (C) personal rights
    (D) school

70. (A) teaching
    (B) profession
    (C) learning
    (D) process

Questions 71 to 80

In the _____ for better _____ skills,
         71   72

many companies, followed by several _____
                                        73

of the armed _____, have sponsored listen-
              74

ing seminars. The _____ of listening as a
                   75

learned skill has _____ filtered down
                   76

through the U.S. educational _____. Con-
                              77

gress has added speaking and _____ to the
                              78

three Rs as _____ skills to be _____ in
             79   80

the public schools.

71. (A) horror
    (B) quest
    (C) wish
    (D) job

72. (A) listening
    (B) speaking
    (C) basic
    (D) upgraded

73. (A) areas
    (B) captains
    (C) generals
    (D) branches

74. (A) guards
    (B) forest
    (C) services
    (D) men

75. (A) good
    (B) promise
    (C) way
    (D) idea

76. (A) slowly
    (B) not
    (C) never
    (D) always

77. (A) branches
    (B) system
    (C) colleges
    (D) methods

78. (A) talking
    (B) hearing
    (C) listening
    (D) mathematics

79. (A) basic
    (B) new
    (C) viable
    (D) popular

80. (A) used
    (B) proved
    (C) held
    (D) taught

PROFESSIONAL KNOWLEDGE
150 Minutes–80 Questions

Directions: Choose the best answer for each question and blacken the corresponding space on the Answer Sheet for Sample Test 3. The correct answers and the explanations follow the test.

1. Which of the following is the most effective way of introducing a topic?

   (A) lecture
   (B) discussion

2. The major benefit of parent-school committees is that

   (A) parents feel part of the school
   (B) teachers don't have to do all the work

3. The school district has proposed a new program. It will be most successful if the people involved in it are

   (A) teachers only, so that it will be run most efficiently
   (B) teachers and parents
   (C) teachers, parents and community

4. The purpose of norm-referenced tests is

   (A) to find out if the students are normal
   (B) to find out what percent of the questions the students got right
   (C) to compare the students with other similar students

5. Jaime scored 60 on a percentile-ranked test. This means that

   (A) 60% of the students taking the test scored higher than Jaime
   (B) 60% of the students taking the test scored lower than Jaime
   (C) Jaime got 60% of the questions right
   (D) Jaime got 60% of the questions wrong

6. When explaining percentile-ranked tests to the public, it is important to state

I. what group took the test
II. that the scores show how students performed in relation to other students
III. that the scores show how students performed according to an absolute measure

   (A) I
   (B) I and II
   (C) I, II and III
   (D) II and III

7. Parent-teacher conferences should be

   (A) scheduled for the convenience of the teacher
   (B) scheduled for the convenience of the parents
   (C) scheduled for the mutual convenience of the teacher and parents

8. Parent-teacher conferences should cover

   (A) problems the student is experiencing
   (B) successes the student has had
   (C) over-all progress

9. Testing is used to

   (A) comply with state requirements
   (B) satisfy parents' concerns
   (C) evaluate students' progress

10. If a teacher wants to let a child know that he has done well, the best way is to

    (A) write a note and place it in his folder
    (B) write a note to be taken home
    (C) tell him he has done well

11. If a child is to be spanked (consistent with state law and school board policy), the teacher should inform the

    (A) principal
    (B) principal and counselor
    (C) principal, counselor and parents
    (D) parent

12. A teacher needs to use good planning and management of time in order to

    (A) leave the school at a reasonable time in the afternoon
    (B) cover all the material she has planned

13. An advantage of weekly or monthly staff meetings is

    (A) learning peers' concerns and news of the school and district
    (B) camaraderie
    (C) learning what is on the weekly bulletin

14. It is beneficial for a teacher who is new to a school to

    (A) keep to herself for a time until she is confident
    (B) get to know a few teachers who have the same type of class
    (C) get to know as many of the teachers and support staff as possible

15. "The students will be able to spell forty words with 95% accuracy." This is a (an)

    (A) goal
    (B) objective
    (C) evaluation
    (D) concept

16. The major advantage of competency-based instruction is that

    (A) both teacher and students will know what the goal is and when the goal has been reached
    (B) goals are stated in concrete terms
    (C) lesson plans don't have to be rewritten continually

17. A lesson plan is a major tool for a teacher in
    I. time management
    II. progress evaluation
    III. contingencies, such as illness

    (A) I, II and III
    (B) III
    (C) II and III
    (D) I and III

18. To involve your class in the democratic process, you would

    (A) let the students plan the next unit to be studied
    (B) let the students present the next unit to be studied
    (C) have a class discussion on what the students would like to learn from the unit

19. Students who are not familiar with standardized tests are likely

    (A) to score lower than what their actual ability is
    (B) accidentally to score better than what their actual ability is

20. A student's score on a test could be skewed by
    I. emotional variations (happiness or grief)
    II. anxiety
    III. physical variations (hunger or lack of sleep)
    IV. surroundings (strange place, noise, heat)

    (A) I, II and III
    (B) I, III and IV
    (C) II, III and IV
    (D) I, II, III and IV

21. Some subjects need to be taught sequentially (one step after another), while others lend themselves to being taught in discrete units. Which of the following subjects is (are) best taught sequentially?

    (A) history
    (B) algebra
    (C) literature
    (D) history and algebra

22. As students get older, differences in their achievement levels

    (A) lessen
    (B) increase

23. In judging students' performance in school, teachers should

    (A) be alert to influences outside school that may affect students' performance
    (B) not allow outside influences to sway their judgment

24. A student who can't remember ever failing a test, even though he has failed many, is coping through

    (A) projection
    (B) regression
    (C) repression
    (D) sublimation

25. When talking in the presence of a child, one should

    (A) talk about him
    (B) talk directly to him
    (C) ignore him

26. If the answer to a question a child asks is beyond his comprehension, it is best to

    (A) tell him that the answer is too difficult
    (B) answer his question even if he won't understand

27. Students' scores on a test were 72, 72, 73, 74, 76, 78, 81, 83, 85. A score of 76 is the

    (A) mean
    (B) median
    (C) mode
    (D) average

28. A multiple-choice question should have from _____ answers.

    (A) 1 to 7
    (B) 2 to 6
    (C) 3 to 5
    (D) 3 to 7

29. In administering a standardized test, great care must be taken to

    (A) follow the proscribed format
    (B) allow for individual student differences
    (C) explain everything in great detail

30. To test students' mastery of mathematics, the most appropriate test is

    (A) multiple-choice format
    (B) true-or-false questions
    (C) completion questions
    (D) essay format

31. A student must write a term paper for both his history class and his literature class. He chooses a topic that is satisfactory to both teachers. Should he be allowed to write only one term paper?

    (A) yes
    (B) no

32. Sources a teacher can use to find appropriate resources for teaching are
    I. school or county media centers
    II. libraries
    III. public agencies
    IV. people in the community

    (A) I, II and III
    (B) II, III and IV
    (C) I, III and IV
    (D) I, II, III and IV

33. After a test on a unit has been given and recorded, the teacher should

    (A) go on to the next unit
    (B) go over the test and explain any questions the students may have
    (C) announce everyone's scores

34. Mainstreaming is the practice of

    (A) teaching the same thing to everyone
    (B) "tracking" students
    (C) grouping students according to ability
    (D) integrating handicapped students into the regular classroom

35. Having a mock presidential election, complete with debates, discussion of issues and voting, teaches students

    (A) the decision-making process
    (B) whether they would like to be politicians or not
    (C) whether to be a Democrat or a Republican

36. The most important fact for a teacher to know about learning methods is

    (A) that she should find the one method that suits her style
    (B) that all of them must be used
    (C) that no one method will work for all students

37. Typing is a subject that lends itself to

    (A) concept teaching
    (B) task teaching
    (C) generalization teaching
    (D) inference and conclusion teaching

38. A person's basic character is generally set by the time she is how many years old?

    (A) 6
    (B) 10
    (C) 18
    (D) 25

39. The teacher who believes that her students should pursue their separate interests on a topic would find the learning results to be

    (A) similar
    (B) successful
    (C) progressive
    (D) inconsistent

40. The best discipline of students is

    (A) benevolently authoritarian
    (B) militaristic
    (C) democratic
    (D) self-motivated

41. Anecdotal records should be used to

    (A) prepare for discipline of a student
    (B) keep a record of a student's grades
    (C) protect the teacher, if necessary
    (D) provide material that may explain a student's behavior

42. Which is less effective in motivating a student?

    (A) ignoring him
    (B) reprimanding him

43. If classes were to be grouped homogeneously, then

    (A) students of widely different abilities would be in the same class
    (B) this would be termed "mainstreaming"
    (C) students of similar ability would be in the same class
    (D) there would be no heterogeneous students in the class

44. Homework in the elementary grades is primarily used

    (A) for punishment
    (B) for reinforcement
    (C) to accustom children to the idea of homework
    (D) to make children feel important

45. Memorization in school is justified when

    (A) it results in a convenience or pleasure for the learner
    (B) it demonstrates the power of the mind
    (C) it demonstrates the discipline of the mind
    (D) it is used as punishment

46. If all of the students in a class passed the pre-test for a unit, the teacher should

    (A) go through the lesson quickly
    (B) administer the post-test
    (C) go through the unit as usual
    (D) go on to the next unit

47. Asking questions in class is best done by

    (A) asking the question, then calling on a particular student
    (B) calling on a particular student, then asking the question

48. At which level of government lies the primary responsibility for schools?

    (A) federal
    (B) state
    (C) county
    (D) local

49. It is hard to tell whether a student is guessing or not on a _____ test.

    (A) multiple-choice
    (B) completion
    (C) matching
    (D) true-or-false
    (E) essay

50. If a teacher wants to know whether the students completely understand a concept in high school social science, the test he would use would be

    (A) multiple-choice

(B) completion
(C) matching
(D) true-or-false
(E) essay

51. You want students to identify presidents of the United States with their administrations, so the test you use is

(A) multiple-choice
(B) completion
(C) matching
(D) true-or-false
(E) essay

52. Programmed learning material would be most likely to be found in

(A) a class divided in three groups
(B) independent study
(C) a class in which the teacher tries to individualize the instruction

53. It is possible that some children who are good readers in the early grades are merely

(A) quiet
(B) trying to please teacher and parents
(C) interested in the reading material
(D) myopic

54. A student will usually remember what he has learned if it is

(A) important for a test
(B) repeated
(C) interesting to him

55. Jonathan doesn't learn anything he hears; he must see it to remember it. In order to facilitate learning, he could

(A) use a computer
(B) read supplementary textbooks
(C) take notes and study them
(D) all of the above

56. One time that Sharon takes an IQ test, her score is 103. The next time it is 99. You conclude that

(A) Sharon's intelligence is decreasing
(B) Sharon didn't try as hard on the second test
(C) the scores are not significantly different

57. Lesson plans

(A) are a formality and a waste of time
(B) should be strictly adhered to
(C) should be flexible

58. Movies shown in the classroom

(A) fill up time
(B) are a waste of time
(C) are most effective if followed by discussion

59. Team teaching

(A) is a waste of taxpayers' money
(B) makes the best use of both teachers' talents
(C) is going out of style
(D) is a new concept in teaching

60. Jeff is a second grader who continually pushes and shoves other children. His teacher says, "He cannot keep his hands to himself." What can the teacher suspect as the cause of Jeff's behavior?

(A) Jeff has been mistreated at home.
(B) Jeff needs the companionship of other children.
(C) Jeff is a bully.

61. Boys in elementary school need a great deal of physical action. To fulfill this need in the classroom, a teacher could

(A) have the class make models of what is being studied
(B) have the children act out stories
(C) have spelling and arithmetic relay races
(D) have two-minute stretching and running-in-place breaks every hour
(E) all of the above

62. A student is having behavior problems in class. The teacher should discuss the problem and possible solutions with the following people in which order?

(A) principal, counselor, parents, student
(B) parents, counselor, student, principal
(C) counselor, student, principal, student
(D) student, parents, counselor, principal
(E) student, counselor, principal, parents

63. The greatest influence on a child is

    (A) the school environment
    (B) his or her peers
    (C) the home environment

64. Forty-year-olds have slightly less ability to learn than do twenty-year-olds. However, as many college-age students have learned to their dismay, older students do learn as well if not better than their younger counterparts. The difference between innate ability and performance can be attributed to

    (A) motivation
    (B) interest
    (C) attention
    (D) better use of available time
    (E) all of the above

65. Recently increased community involvement in schools was a result of

    (A) interest in schools
    (B) encouragement by school districts
    (C) dissatisfaction with the schools

66. The most prominent educational issue of the mid 1980s is

    (A) accountability
    (B) busing
    (C) mainstreaming
    (D) Headstart
    (E) bilingual education

67. The most publicized educational report in the early 1980s was

    (A) *Johnny Still Can't Read*
    (B) *José Can't Read*
    (C) *Educational Excellence*
    (D) *A Nation at Risk*
    (E) *Bilingualism in America*

68. One measure of accountability implemented by many states is

    (A) entrance tests for high school
    (B) exit tests from high school
    (C) entrance tests for colleges
    (D) exit tests from colleges

69. Some class activities require quiet behavior on the part of the students, while at other times more liveliness is warranted. What would be your criterion of inappropriate student behavior in a classroom?

    (A) how often the student had done this before
    (B) whether the student was at his or her desk
    (C) the level of loudness of the student
    (D) whether the behavior was disruptive to other students

70. As a result of reports showing American students lagging behind students in other countries in education, American educators are now stressing

    (A) the study of foreign languages
    (B) educational excellence
    (C) exchange programs
    (D) double homework
    (E) fewer extracurricular activities

71. Which is more important for learning to occur?

    (A) readiness
    (B) training

72. When corporal punishment is to be administered, it is best to

    (A) spank in the privacy of an empty classroom to save the child embarrassment
    (B) spank in the principal's office
    (C) let the principal do the spanking
    (D) have a witness and inform the parents and the principal

73. What can a teacher do for students in his class who are not on grade level?

    (A) give them materials on their level and let them work at a pace that is reasonable for them, trying to bring them up to grade level
    (B) give them the same work as the other students, only not so much, so that they won't feel embarrassed
    (C) give them the same work as the other students, because they will absorb as much as they are capable of

74. The best way to get students interested in a new topic, such as camping, is to

    (A) tell them about your camping experiences
    (B) ask a forest ranger to talk about camping
    (C) show the class a film about camping
    (D) ask them to relate their camping experiences

75. Showing one student's grades to another student

    (A) is not professional
    (B) creates the incentive for the student to improve
    (C) should be done only in certain circumstances

Questions 76 to 78

You have recently given a test to your sophomore biology class. The grades were low, and the students claim that the test was unfair.

76. What should you do?

    (A) Check the test to see whether their claim is valid.
    (B) Increase everyone's score by one grade.
    (C) Dismiss this as sour grapes.
    (D) Report the students who complained to the vice-principal.

77. What could cause your test to be unfair?

    (A) The test included items not in the readings or lectures.
    (B) The test items were primarily on peripheral matter.
    (C) The test was too long.
    (D) all of the above

78. What can you do to assure that your tests are fair?

    (A) Ask each student to submit one question.
    (B) Write twenty questions for the test, and let each student answer any ten of the questions.
    (C) Make all of the questions true or false.
    (D) Use the objectives for the unit as the guide for the test.

79. An integrated curriculum

    (A) emphasizes to the students the interrelationship of the courses they are studying
    (B) bases the curriculum on the various ethnic cultures of the students
    (C) has students of various ethnic backgrounds on the curriculum development committee

80. An error frequently made about children is

    (A) overestimating their intellect
    (B) overestimating their need for rest
    (C) underestimating their need for rest
    (D) underestimating their intellect

ANSWERS TO SAMPLE TEST 3

BASIC SKILLS

Mathematics

1. A	11. B	21. C	31. B	41. D
2. B	12. B	22. C	32. C	42. B
3. D	13. A	23. D	33. C	43. B
4. D	14. B	24. D	34. B	44. A
5. C	15. B	25. C	35. B	45. B
6. B	16. C	26. D	36. A	46. A
7. C	17. B	27. B	37. C	47. B
8. C	18. D	28. B	38. C	48. B
9. B	19. D	29. A	39. B	49. D
10. B	20. C	30. A	40. A	50. C

Reading

1. A	17. B	33. A	49. A	65. A
2. D	18. C	34. C	50. D	66. D
3. A	19. A	35. A	51. D	67. A
4. B	20. D	36. D	52. A	68. D
5. D	21. A	37. A	53. B	69. D
6. C	22. B	38. B	54. B	70. B
7. C	23. D	39. C	55. C	71. B
8. A	24. B	40. D	56. A	72. A
9. B	25. D	41. B	57. D	73. D
10. D	26. A	42. C	58. C	74. C
11. C	27. C	43. D	59. A	75. D
12. A	28. C	44. A	60. B	76. A
13. D	29. D	45. B	61. C	77. B
14. B	30. A	46. C	62. A	78. C
15. A	31. B	47. D	63. D	79. A
16. A	32. A	48. C	64. B	80. D

PROFESSIONAL KNOWLEDGE

1. B	17. A	33. B	49. D	65. C
2. A	18. C	34. D	50. E	66. A
3. C	19. A	35. A	51. C	67. D
4. C	20. D	36. C	52. B	68. B
5. B	21. D	37. B	53. D	69. D
6. B	22. B	38. B	54. C	70. B
7. C	23. A	39. D	55. D	71. A
8. C	24. C	40. D	56. C	72. D
9. C	25. B	41. D	57. C	73. A
10. C	26. B	42. A	58. C	74. D
11. C	27. B	43. C	59. B	75. A
12. B	28. C	44. C	60. B	76. A
13. A	29. A	45. A	61. E	77. D
14. C	30. C	46. D	62. E	78. D
15. B	31. A	47. A	63. C	79. A
16. A	32. D	48. B	64. E	80. D

EXPLANATION OF ANSWERS TO SAMPLE TEST 3

BASIC SKILLS

MATHEMATICS

1. **A** rate × time = distance. *Or* distance ÷ rate = time
   Beth: 300 miles ÷ 60 mph = 5 hours
   Kay: 300 miles ÷ 50 mph = 6 hours
   Beth will arrive 6 − 5 = 1 hour sooner than Kay

2. **B** Harry edits ¼ + ¼ = ½ of the book the first two weeks in May. Harry has 1 − ½ = ½ of the book left to edit. He will have to edit ½ of 180 = 90 pages in the next two weeks.
   $$90 \div 2 = 45 \text{ pages each week}$$

3. **D** $-6 - (+9) =$
   $-6 - \quad 9 = -15$

4. **D** You add deposits; subtract checks and service charges.

5. **C** Use your answer sheet to line up the figures.

6. **B** 15 + 20 + 45 + 65 + 80 + 70 + 55 + 62(+ or −) + 30 + 18(+ or −) = 460

7. **C** $\dfrac{460}{10 \text{ months}} = 46$ 45 is closest

8. **C** It will be less than ¹⁄₁₀ of his annual salary. Eliminate A, B and D.
   $$\frac{\$18,408.00}{12} = \$1,534.00$$

9. **B** Since 231 divides evenly into 173, 712, there is no remainder.

10. **B** In division, *quotient* means answer. Estimate.
    $$\frac{5,600}{40} = \text{about } 140$$

11. **B** The score will be near the middle. Eliminate A.
    $$73 + 75 + 78 + 79 + 81 = 386$$
    $$386 \div 5 = 77\tfrac{1}{5}$$

12. **B** Eliminate D immediately. Align your columns and decimals carefully when you add the monthly balances.
    ```
       $1,024.57
        1,246.85
           30.47
          117.61
          351.13
          573.37
        1,994.55
           65.76
        1,708.84
        2,007.92
        3,462.01
    +   1,280.09
    ```
    $13,863.17   Eliminate C

    $\dfrac{\$13,863.17}{12} = \$1,155.26\tfrac{5}{12}$

13. **A** Subtract. 11 lb 5 oz
    ```
                  − 7 lb 7 oz
    ```
    Borrow. (1 lb = 16 oz)
    11 lb 5 oz = 10 lb 21 oz
    ```
                − 7 lb  7 oz
                  3 lb 14 oz
    ```

14. **B** Area = 17 × 27 = 459 sq ft
    9 sq ft = 1 sq yd

    $$\frac{459}{9} = 51 \text{ sq yd}$$

15. **B** 51 × $9 = $459

16. **C** First, estimate: 3,000
    ```
                            1,000
                           62,000
                            1,000
                            1,000
                           68,000  Eliminate D
    ```

148

Align the numbers.

$$\begin{array}{r} 2,745 \\ 839 \\ 62,487 \\ 987 \\ + 1,247 \\ \hline \ldots 05 \end{array}$$

This is as far as you need to add in order to decide on the correct answer.

17. **B**

$$\begin{array}{r} 9,850 \\ - 7,970 \\ \hline 1,880 \end{array}$$

18. **D** Estimate. $30 \times 17 = 510$

19. **D**

17⅝	Change to eighths:	17⅝
⅛		⅛
⅞		⅞
1½		1⅘
¾		⅚
+ ⅜		+ ⅜

$$18\ ^{26}/_{8} = 21¼$$

20. **C**

$$\begin{array}{rl} \$ 595 & \text{price} \\ - 85 & \text{down payment} \\ \hline \$ 510 & \text{amount to be financed} \end{array} \quad \frac{\$510}{30} = \$17$$

21. **C**

$$\begin{array}{r} 4,576 \\ 1,379 \\ 3,597 \end{array}$$

Suzanne flew 9,552 miles

$$\begin{array}{r} 10,000 \\ - 9,552 \\ \hline 448 \quad \text{miles left} \end{array}$$

22. **C** $\dfrac{is}{of}$ $\dfrac{98 \times 100}{35} = 280$

23. **D** $\dfrac{1}{2} - \dfrac{1}{3} = \dfrac{1 \times 3}{2 \times 3} - \dfrac{1 \times 2}{3 \times 2} = \dfrac{3 - 2}{6} = \dfrac{1}{6}$

24. **D**

Plus: balance	$ 107.52	*Minus:* check	$57.61
deposit	452.63	check	47.16
	$ 560.15	service charge	9.70
			$ 114.47

$$\begin{array}{r} \$ 560.15 \\ - 114.68 \\ \hline \$ 445.68 \quad \text{balance} \end{array}$$

25. **C**

$$\begin{array}{r} \$2.24 \\ .20 = 1\ oz \\ \hline \$2.04 \end{array}$$

$$\frac{\$2.04}{.17} = 12\ oz$$

$$1 + 12 = 13\ oz$$

26. **D** In each case the shaded part is ½ of the whole triangle.
1. ¾ = ½   2. ¾ = ½   3. ³⁄₆ = ½
4. ⅛ = ½

27. **B** ⅝ × ⅗ = ⅜

28. **B** ⅝ − ⅜ = ²⁄₈ = ¼

29. **A** You want about ⅓ of $28.65. That is close to $10.
Only A fits.

30. **A** Substitute in the formula. Multiply before adding.

$$\frac{(15 \times 74 + 67 \times 69 + 18 \times 87)}{100} =$$

$$\frac{1,110 + 4,623 + 1,566}{100} =$$

$$\frac{7299}{100} = 72.99$$

31. **B**

$$\begin{array}{r} \$ 127.50 \\ 1,547.05 \\ 57.55 \\ \hline \$1,732.10 \end{array}$$

You will need to add only as far as the 2 to choose the correct answer.

32. **C** $\dfrac{480}{30} = 16$ inches

33. **C** $180 \times ¼ = 45$ pages week 1. $180 - 45 = 135$ pages left
$135 \times ⅓ = 45$ pages week 2. $135 - 45 = 90$ pages left

$$\frac{90}{2} = 45 \text{ pages each week}$$

34. **B** $34 + 34 + 34 + 35 + 37 + 31 = 205$

35. **B**

$$\begin{array}{rl} \$ 5,201.13 & \textbf{income} \\ - 4,896.31 & \textbf{expenses} \\ \hline \$ 304.82 & \textbf{net income} \end{array}$$

36. **A**

		change to twelfths:	
Mon.	$2\frac{3}{4}$		$2\frac{9}{12}$
Tues.	$1\frac{1}{3}$		$1\frac{4}{12}$
Wed.	$1\frac{1}{3}$		$1\frac{4}{12}$
Thurs.	$2\frac{1}{2}$		$2\frac{6}{12}$
Fri.	3		3
			$9\frac{23}{12}$

$9\frac{23}{12} = 9 + 1\frac{11}{12} = 10\frac{11}{12}$ hours

37. **C**

$2.97
1.39
1.27
2.57
1.96
1.34

$11.50

38. **C**

70%
−55%

15%

39. **B** Mark off the length of the scale on the edge of your answer sheet. Lay the edge of your answer sheet along side b and mark on line b where the answer sheet mark is. Repeat as necessary to estimate the length.

40. **A** purchases $ 12.96 money tendered $ 25.00
            8.77   −21.73
         ---------   --------
         $ 21.73 $ 3.27

41. **D**

rectangle $a = l \times w$ triangle $a = \frac{1}{2} h \times b$
           $a = 7 \times 5$ $a = \frac{1}{2} \times 5 \times 6$
           $a = 35$ $a = 15$

Add the areas: $35 + 15 = 50$

42. **B** Do the operation inside the bracket before removing the bracket. Remove brackets from the inside out. This is the opposite of peeling an onion. Do multiplication and division from left to right, then addition and subtraction from left to right.

$7.12 \times [2.3 - (.6 \times 7 - 1.9)] =$
$7.12 \times [2.3 - (4.2 - 1.9)] =$
$7.12 \times [2.3 - 2.3] =$
$7.12 \times [0] = 0$

Anything multiplied by 0 equals 0.

43. **B** $\frac{1}{7} \times \frac{1}{9} = \frac{1}{63}$

44. **A** $178.15 \times 0.06 = 10.689.

45. **B** You can do this in steps:

7 hours $\times$ 186 days = 1302 hours

$1302 \times \frac{2}{7} = \frac{2604}{7} = 372$ hours nonteaching time

$372 \times \frac{1}{15} = 24\frac{4}{5}$ hours spent in meetings

Or you can do it all at once:

7 hours $\times$ 186 days $\times \frac{2}{7} \times \frac{1}{15} = \frac{124}{5} = 24\frac{4}{5}$ hours

46. **A** 1000 grams = 1 kilo

$$\frac{760 \text{ students} \times 100 \text{ grams} \times 2 \text{ hamburgers}}{1,000 \text{ grams}} = 152 \text{ kilos.}$$

47. **B** $7\frac{1}{5} \div \frac{5}{8} = \frac{36}{5} \div \frac{5}{8} = \frac{36}{5} \times \frac{8}{5} = \frac{288}{25} = 11\frac{13}{25}$

48. **B** $\frac{\$ \ 137.50}{\$1,250.00} \times 100 = 11\%$

49. **D**

	Year	Month	Day
	1984	9	9
Borrow (1 mo = 30 days)	1984	8	39
	−1978	11	12
			27 days
Borrow (1 yr = 12 months)	1983	20	
	−1978	11	
	5 yr	9 mo	27 days

50. **C** The shortest route is Spokane–Pullman–Moscow–Sandpoint. Follow the procedure in question 39.

READING

1–10.

One of the things that new teachers or <u>teachers</u> in a
                                           1
new situation fear is losing control of the <u>class</u>. Letting
                                              2
a class have group discussion or break into <u>groups</u> for
                                              3
an activity <u>involves</u> a certain <u>amount</u> of abdication of
             4   5
control and trust in the group. Without this, however,

few teachers can <u>attain</u> a high level of <u>goal</u> achieve-
                  6   7
ment. How this important facet of <u>teaching</u> is to be
                                    8
<u>approached</u> is the subject of <u>considerable</u> discussion
9   10
and debate.

11–20.

Many teachers who <u>advocate</u> involvement say that it
11
makes a class more <u>interesting</u>. It seems to make the
12
time go faster and make a class less boring. It <u>forces</u>
13
students to concentrate on the <u>subject</u>. They can't
14
"tune out." There <u>are</u> many other reasons given for
15
involvement, but the only <u>reason</u> that <u>it</u> should be used
16   17
is that it is the best method <u>of</u> accomplishing the
18
specific learning goal. This criterion should be used in
19
deciding whether to use any <u>teaching</u> technique.
20

21–30.

Adults can learn from listening to <u>lectures</u>, but they are
21
more likely to <u>learn</u> from discussion. Since nearly all
22
<u>adult</u> learning is self-directed, why do some not
23
<u>participate</u> in discussion? <u>Upon</u> questioning you will
24   25
often find that the <u>nonparticipant</u> thinks that she will be
26
<u>embarrassed</u> and that her ideas are not <u>valuable</u> to the
27   28
group. This person has been trained not to participate,
and until this <u>training</u> is overcome, she will not get the
29
full learning <u>benefits</u> that she should from a teaching
30
session.

31–40.

A recent <u>survey</u> revealed that college students don't
31
think that their <u>professors</u> should be humorous. When
32
questioned <u>further</u>, they said that professors who used
33
humor in the classroom were not projecting the correct
34
image and did not seem to take themselves, the subject
35
or the <u>students</u> seriously enough. Interestingly, though,
36
students <u>remember</u> the serious material the professor
37
using humor presented much <u>better</u> than the material
38
of nonhumorous <u>professors</u>. Could it be that these
39
students think that learning has to be <u>dull</u>?
40

41–50.

Salesmen make a point of <u>learning</u> your name and
41
using it often. Teachers are salesmen of sorts, too.
Think how <u>good</u> it feels when someone remembers
42
your name, and how <u>awful</u> it feels when someone
43
doesn't. It is <u>important</u> to learn your students' names as
44
soon as possible. <u>Greeting</u> each student as he comes
45
into the room, <u>concentrating</u> on his name and using it
46
will help you remember. If the students keep the same
<u>places</u> you will more readily <u>associate</u> the name and the
47   48
face. Try to think of something distinctive that will <u>link</u>
49
the person's face and name. The more often you use a
person's name, the better you will remember it. What
did you say your <u>name</u> is, again?
50

51–60.

How you treat your <u>child</u> at an early age may affect
51
<u>whether</u> he becomes a conformist or an <u>individualist</u>.
52   53
Although <u>parents</u> want their children to be well
54
behaved and <u>compliant</u>, they want the children to grow
55
up to be independent and <u>creative</u>. <u>Parents</u> are influ-
56   57
enced by their own situation. Parents belonging to
lower economic groups who want their children to
<u>succeed</u> will stress conformity as a way to get ahead.
58
Parents who are secure in <u>established</u> society encourage
59
their <u>children</u> to take risks.
60

61–70.

Teacher-education programs have come under much criticism lately. Many critics advocate doing away with
<u>61</u>
all teacher-education classes, substituting courses on
<u>62</u>
the material to be taught. However, the teacher's
<u>63</u>
knowledge of subject matter is of no value to the
<u>64</u>
students unless the teacher can convey it to those
<u>65</u>
students. To do this, the teacher needs to learn about classroom control, grading, various methods of teaching to ensure maximum learning, how to make a lesson
<u>66</u>
interesting and where and how to get appropriate
<u>67</u>
resources. The teacher also needs to know about child and adolescent psychology, school law and the educa-
<u>68</u>   <u>69</u>
tional administrative system. Teacher-education courses are the best way to learn the tools of the profession.
<u>70</u>

71–80.

In the quest for better listening skills, many companies,
<u>71</u>   <u>72</u>
followed by several branches of the armed services,
<u>73</u>   <u>74</u>
have sponsored listening seminars. The idea of listening
<u>75</u>
as a learned skill has slowly filtered down through the
<u>76</u>
U.S. educational system. Congress has added speaking
<u>77</u>
and listening to the three Rs as basic skills to be taught
<u>78</u>   <u>79</u>   <u>80</u>
in the public schools.

PROFESSIONAL KNOWLEDGE

1. **B** Discussion involves students immediately.

2. **A** Parent-school committees develop the involvement of parents.

3. **C** The more people involved, the more successful a project will be.

4. **C** Norm-referenced tests compare students with other students.

5. **B** A student who scored 60% on a percentile-ranked test scored better than 60% of the students taking the test.

6. **B** Identify the norm group and explain the meaning of the score.

7. **C** Scheduling for mutual convenience is best.

8. **C** Parent-teacher conferences are the time to discuss general progress.

9. **C** Testing should evaluate students' progress.

10. **C** Oral praise is most meaningful.

11. **C** Inform all who will be affected.

12. **B** Effective planning helps a teacher accomplish her goals.

13. **A** Faculty meetings provide an opportunity to keep abreast of what is happening.

14. **C** The sooner you know all the people who make a school run, the better.

15. **B** An objective states a desired result in concrete terms.

16. **A** Competency-based instruction clarifies goals and objectives.

17. **A** A lesson plan helps with time management, progress evaluation and substitute teaching.

18. **C** Democracy in the classroom is not turning control of the class over to the students but involving them in the educational process.

19. **A** Students who are unfamiliar with standardized tests are at a disadvantage compared with students who are used to them.

20. **D** Students' scores can be affected by any number of variables.

21. **D** History and algebra are suitable for sequential teaching.

22. **B** As students mature, their achievement levels vary more.

23. **A** Teachers should be alert to outside problems students may have that can impair progress.

24. **C** Repression is forgetting something painful.

25. **B** Children, like adults, should be treated politely, like human beings. Talking about them as though they were statues is rude.

26. **B** Answer children's questions. It is amazing how much they understand.

27. **B** The median is the middle score when the scores are arranged in progressive numerical order.

28. **C** Three to five answer choices provide adequate variety.

29. **A** The validity of standardized tests depends on the tests being administered identically.

30. **C** Completion questions (find the answer) best test mathematical skills.

31. **A** If one term paper will suffice, it is pointless to write two. The second one would become mere busy work.

32. **D** A teacher should draw on the widest possible range of resources available. It improves the program and fosters community involvement.

33. **B** If the teacher doesn't go over the test and explain the answers, the students don't learn from the test.

34. **D** Mainstreaming is an effort to provide as normal surroundings as possible for handicapped students.

35. **A** Participation in mock elections teaches students about a facet of the decision-making process.

36. **C** A teacher's job has been described as teaching the same thing seven different ways. Children learn in a variety of ways.

37. **B** Typing is a task that students learn primarily by doing.

38. **B** It is generally considered that a child's character is formed before the age of 10.

39. **D** Students need direction in their learning in order for a base amount of similar learning to take place.

40. **D** Self-motivated discipline is what society strives for.

41. **D** Anecdotal records, detailed records of a student's behavior over a period of time, should be used to shed light on that behavior.

42. **A** Ignoring a student does not motivate him.

43. **C** Homogeneous grouping is the grouping of students of like achievement levels.

44. **C** Teachers try to prepare their students for what is ahead by giving them small amounts of homework.

45. **A** Learning poems can be a pleasure and learning the multiplication tables is a convenience.

46. **D** If the students pass the pre-test, they obviously know the material, and the unit need not be taught.

47. **A** If the students don't know who will be called on to answer, then all the students will pay attention to the question.

48. **B** The individual states have the primary responsibility for education.

49. **D** A student has a 50% chance of guessing correctly on a true-false test. This type of test lends itself most to guessing.

50. **E** A student can explain why he thinks as he does on an essay test.

51. **C** Matching tests are useful in history, geography and science, where categories exist that can be matched.

52. **B** Programmed learning materials were designed for individual study.

53. **D** Myopic children tend to be good readers because they focus well at close range, as for reading, and not at long range.

54. **C** We learn most readily those things that we are interested in.

55. **D** All the choices would reinforce his visual learning.

56. **C** The four-point difference is not significant.

57. **C** Lesson plans are guides, and should be used as such.

58. **C** Discussion solidifies students' thinking after seeing a movie or performance.

59. **B** Team teaching can use the best abilities of both teachers. One may be a musician, the other an artist. The children receive the benefits of both their talents.

60. **B** Jeff may need the closeness of companionship. He is trying to get it but doesn't know how to do it in an acceptable manner.

61. **E** All of the suggestions use physical energy in the learning process.

62. **E** The teacher should try to solve the problem at the lowest level. If the problem is resolved at any stage, he should not proceed to the next stage.

63. **C** The home has the most influence on a child.

64. **E** Older adults may have more motivation to learn and interest in the subject, pay more attention and make better use of their time. This more than makes up for any lessening in their ability to learn.

65. **C** Dissatisfaction with schools has increased community involvement and caused new laws to be passed and stricter standards to be enforced.

66. **A** Accountability is the most prominent recent educational issue. The other choices were current earlier than accountability.

67. **D** *A Nation at Risk* was the report of the Andrew Carnegie Foundation on the decline in American education.

68. **B** Exit tests from high school have been implemented by many school districts and states.

69. **D** If behavior is disruptive to other students it is inappropriate.

70. **B** Excellence in education is being emphasized in a variety of ways.

71. **A** Readiness and training are both important, but without readiness, training is useless.

72. **D** A witness is necessary to protect the teacher, and the sooner the teacher informs both the principal and the parents, the better.

73. **A** Students learn best when they can succeed at their own level.

74. **D** Students are interested when they participate and when what they contribute is considered important.

75. **A** A student's grades are confidential.

76. **A** Perhaps the students' claim is valid.

77. **D** Tests should reflect both the material that was to be studied and the time allotted for completing the tests.

78. **D** Using the unit objectives as a guide for the test ensures that you will test what you have taught and that the test will reflect the objectives of the unit.

79. **A** An integrated curriculum is designed to connect all the subjects so that the students will understand their relationship. No subject is an island unto itself.

80. **D** People often underestimate children's intelligence.